PREDICTIONS 2017
AQUARIUS

Karmel Nair was born a Catholic, is married to a Hindu and practises the Buddhist way of life. Tarot happened by chance when she was pursuing a successful career as a radio jockey. Karmel discovered her intuitive powers as she delved deep into Tarot, and went on to become one of Mumbai's leading Tarot readers. The Tarot journey helped her discover Vipassana, the study and practice of mindfulness and she turned to meditation. Equipped with a master's degree in Psychotherapy and her skill as a Tarot reader, Karmel realized she could help people know what the future had in store for them and to mitigate the negatives through corrective measures. *Predictions 2017: Aquarius*, a product of Karmel's experience, learning and understanding of Tarot, is not only a book of the future, but also a medium to change it through spiritual realization by harnessing the power of the Being – present-moment awareness.

D1050213

PREDICTIONS
2017

AQUARIUS
21 JANUARY – 18 FEBRUARY

KARMEL NAIR

First published in India in 2016 by Harlequin
An imprint of HarperCollins *Publishers*

Copyright © Karmel Nair 2016

P-ISBN: 978-93-5029-421-5
E-ISBN: 978-93-5029-422-2

2 4 6 8 10 9 7 5 3 1

Karmel Nair asserts the moral right
to be identified as the author of this work.

HarperCollins *Publishers*
A-75, Sector 57, Noida, Uttar Pradesh 201301, India
1 London Bridge Street, London, SE1 9GF, United Kingdom
Hazelton Lanes, 55 Avenue Road, Suite 2900, Toronto, Ontario M5R 3L2
and 1995 Markham Road, Scarborough, Ontario M1B 5M8, Canada
25 Ryde Road, Pymble, Sydney, NSW 2073, Australia
195 Broadway, New York, NY 10007, USA

Typeset in 10/12.5 Adobe Garamond
By Saanvi Graphics Noida

Printed and bound at
Thomson Press (India) Ltd

'Om mani padme hum'

'With constant practice of mindfulness, you can transform the impure body, speech and mind into the pure body, speech and mind of a Buddha.'

– From the Web

Contents

Rediscovering Myself While Discovering Tarot

They say the journey of a thousand miles begins with a single step. There I was on a pleasant evening in Goa in a bustling flea market. The stall in front of me was nondescript yet alluring with bold letters inviting visitors with 'KNOW YOUR DESTINY WITH TAROT'. I took the initial step with trepidation, curiosity and a keenness to know what was in store for me. I entered the stall and met an elderly lady whose hypnotic and magical eyes belied her age. I took the chair in front of her. She immediately asked me in a confident tone, 'What would you like to know?' Well, this was my first time and I was a total novice at asking questions about my future. With all my inexperience and innocence, I gathered courage and came up with a simple question, 'What do you see in my near future?' She shuffled her cards, a total of five, some three or four times and spread them in a circular shape. They looked colourful and interesting, even magical and mystical. She seemed lost in the cards and this kind of generated mixed feelings in me. Was it good or bad? In any case I butted into the silence and asked, 'So what do you see?' To this she answered, 'My dear, I am happy to tell you that I see you getting married to your boyfriend, the one you are seeing now, in less than a year.'

This came as a surprise to me as I was unsure of my ongoing relationship and definitely wasn't considering marriage anytime soon. The other things she said really appalled me. 'I see a new beginning,' she said, 'a beautiful one, but this comes at a price.' I was sold. 'What beginning and what price?' I asked.

'I see you starting a journey that you have never taken before, a journey that will change your life and your life's purpose, but at a price that you may have to pay now. The price is at the cost of your existing job. You may be asked to leave what you believe is your dream job, only to begin the real journey of your life.'

This disappointed me. I loved my job as a radio jockey with a leading radio station; I was doing exceedingly well and there was talk of me being moved to prime time, which was like an indirect promotion. It was out of the question that I would be asked to leave. What journey was I going to start? This didn't go down too well with me. However, with this I ended my reading and bid adieu to the mystical woman.

When I returned to my job, everything looked good, as it was. It continued in the same manner for a couple of days only for something strange to happen after that. In less than ten days I was asked to leave from my present profile and this at a time when I was doing very well and hoping to shift into drive time shows. The project I was working on had moved to some other location and they didn't need me any longer. This shattered me and my dream. That's when the Tarot reader's predictions rang like a warning bell in my head. Her predictions were coming true. I felt it deep in my heart. Four months from the time I got my first ever Tarot reading, I was engaged to my boyfriend and was married after another three months.

Today I am happily married, leading a different but remarkable life in which I discover myself each day. Everything she predicted became true and I found it difficult to accept this, to even acknowledge it. After a couple of months I went back looking for her because the urge to know what she had left unsaid nagged me. She had mentioned a new journey. What could it be? I went back to Goa where I met her at the same place. Luckily for me, I met her just as she was packing up for Europe permanently. I reminded her that I had been there a few months ago and she had predicted everything correctly but with one undisclosed thread of events. 'You will discover yourself through your instinct and intuition. You are meant to do something related to foretelling the destiny of others. Your calling is to see the unknown.' Her prediction was still ambiguous. On the way back I continued to ponder over her words.

Life got back to normal as usual. I found myself a new job, was getting ready to move on with marriage and the rest, but there were sudden incidents that would bring me back to what the Tarot reader had predicted about my self-discovery. Two of my common friends got engaged; I had a nagging feeling about the impending marriage and would often discuss the uncomfortable instinct with my husband. I strongly felt that their marriage wouldn't last long. Since it was only a feeling, an intuition, I couldn't take it beyond discussing it with my husband. My friends got married and three months later they separated. This didn't come as a surprise to me for I knew something was wrong, my instinct had told me so. After a while I predicted India's victory in a critical match, a victory which seemed impossible. Again it was my intuition, my sixth sense. It didn't stop at this. I continued predicting big and small incidents as if my ability had suddenly assumed a mind of its own. A colleague of mine was going through a difficult financial situation; I predicted an unexpected sum of money for him, a windfall. Of course he didn't believe me when I said help would come; I didn't know from where or how, but I knew it would, and it did. Incidents like these would keep bringing me back to the Tarot reader's prediction and that's when it dawned on me that Tarot could be the missing link. Probably this is how I could foretell one's destiny, heal one's life through my knowledge, and show others the way forward. This is when my journey began.

I started working towards this new discovery, the discovery of Tarot. I knew the underlying power of Tarot but the success lay in becoming not just a Tarot reader but a good one. I dedicated my life to its understanding and study. I continued working but only half-heartedly. I was convinced that Tarot was the big change and I had to master it; my destiny rested on it.

There has been no looking back. I have excelled at my work as an expert on this subject and in fact Tarot has opened doors to more than what I thought predicting the past, present and future was all about. It showed me the way to spirituality. Spirituality is about connecting with your real self, with the Being in you. I am yet to get there but the journey has begun. Tarot has opened the door to achieving greatness and success beyond the material wonders of life.

Around this time, Vipassana also happened to me. Vipassana is a scientific form of meditation that releases negative energy from your body and brings your biggest formidable opponent under your complete control, your Mind! I attended a ten-day course of Vipassana, and this opened my third eye. I knew my purpose in life – to reach out to others and guide them to their destiny through Tarot. I studied the science of Psychotherapy and Counselling and this equipped me with a deep and scientific understanding of the human mind and enabled me to understand my clients' needs beyond just pure Tarot reading.

Today Tarot is an intrinsic part of my life and my experience as a Tarot reader gives me the confidence and knowledge to write this book. It is not just a medium to predict the future but a different way of life. As a student and practitioner of Tarot I have learnt that there is more to an individual than just his/

her future. My experience over the years has shown me it is not just the readings that draw people back to me but the whole process of change that Tarot offers. Besides readings, Tarot gives you a new way to handle life by guiding you not only through predictions for the future but also by equipping you with the means to address this future by harnessing your spiritual powers. Tarot is thus the trilogy – it is the future, the medium to change the future and a way to spirituality.

More About Tarot

Tarot is a set of 78 cards believed to have predictive powers. When in contact with the reader's psychic powers, these cards become a tool that can reveal your past and present and predict your future. In the olden days, Tarot was not used as a tool to foretell one's destiny; it got its occult value much later. Tarot is useful in many ways. In my long practice and experience of reading the future of people, I have come upon three most important ways in which Tarot can help you. This book of future is based upon these three aspects of Tarot. Let us begin to unfold the potential of Tarot with the first and most popular benefit.

Tarot as a Medium for Prediction

This is the first and most important aspect of Tarot, as also the most attractive. Based on the reader's potential, Tarot can predict your entire future in a single sitting. Clients typically come to me with their problems, issues or confusions and Tarot offers them a sneak peek into what awaits them with respect to their questions. This prepares them for the better or for worse. To explain this better let me narrate a few real-life stories.

. I had a client who visited me just once. It's difficult to forget her because of the condition she was in when she met me to ask about her marriage. She was thirty-six-years old, had a string of failed relationships and had lost faith in finding the right match for herself. Her parents were desperately seeking a bridegroom for her through various arranged marriage portals. She was convinced that because of her age her chances at marriage were bleak. When she came to me she was dejected, lost and tired; the process of making her past relationships last and the ongoing process of finding a bridegroom had drained her completely. She wanted to know if she would ever get married and live happily.

My reading of her cards showed marriage within six months. Unbelievable as it sounded to her at that time, she took the reading with a pinch of salt. A few months later, I received an e-mail from her. She was getting married and that too, within the time I had predicted. In this instance, Tarot served purely as a tool to predict the client's future.

In another case, I was often visited by a client who had just one question: he wished to buy an apartment of his own in Mumbai. His salary was meagre but this was his only dream and vision. On reading his cards, I told him it would be another two years before he could fulfil his desire. To my dismay, he wouldn't believe me. He often visited me to crosscheck this probability and Tarot's accuracy as his finances dipped or improved. Given his financial position, this seemed a far cry. Believe it or not, two years later, he succeeded in buying his dream apartment on his own merit. The prediction was as true as his home. Tarot can thus work as a tool purely for future predictions. However, its benefits are not limited to this.

Tarot Gives You the Power to Change Your Reading to Achieve the Desired Results

Tarot's potential is not limited to merely predicting your future or reading the past. It goes beyond that. When a prediction is made by the reader, there is a possibility that the prediction may undergo change and thus become the opposite of what was predicted. This primarily happens because Tarot is the only form of occult or medium which gives you the flexibility to change what you don't like about your reading. When you see something negative predicted for you, you have the time to invest the effort and energy to bring about a change in the reading and achieve the desired results. Tarot thus gives you the power to change your life and shape it the way you want to. It will show you where you stand at the present moment and what your future looks like considering your present actions and aura. If you like it, keep it the way it is; if not, change it by changing your actions before the predictions manifest themselves. Tarot therefore serves as a guideline to show you what you can do to improve your future by changing your present. Some of my clients feel happy when their readings go wrong, because the ultimate outcome was what they originally desired.

Three years ago, I had a client who was studying chartered accountancy (CA) and was preparing for his intermediate exams. He was confident when he came to me; his questions revolved around the jobs he would get after completing CA. However, when I did his reading he was shocked. His cards revealed that he would fail his intermediate exams; his plans would undergo a complete downturn. I explained to him that his present efforts weren't enough to help him clear the exam and that instead of dreaming about the future he needed to dedicate all his time and effort to changing the outcome. He called me after six months to tell me that my reading had gone wrong and that he had cleared his exams as he had planned. He thanked me for guiding him and letting him know his true position and potential on the day he had visited me, for helping him address the possibility of failure before it could happen. Tarot showed him his true position and its consequences had he continued in the same vein. A change was needed and Tarot forewarned him about it. Thus, Tarot gives you the power to change your destiny.

You have it all, but the knowing is often amiss. Tarot is the missing link which connects your actions with the desired future.

It tells you what can be done to get from here to where you want to be and not land someplace else, where you don't wish to be.

One of my clients was an excellent worker, ambitious and goal-oriented. She often did readings with me to know about growth and success in her career. However, once she came to me for a different reason. She was given a new role under a new boss. Just before taking over the new role, she had been looking forward to a promotion and a hefty incentive. Apparently, with the new shift and the teething problems with her new boss, she was unsure of her promotion. She wanted a reading primarily to know about her expected promotion. Unfortunately, when I picked her cards, they gave no indication of a promotion. On the contrary, she was set to lose her job! The new boss had taken the decision as he found her overbearing attitude unacceptable. When I told her this she was obviously shocked, but I also informed her that it was in the near future, it hadn't already happened, and she had the time to turn things around by changing her actions and attitude, by working more patiently, approaching work with a modest attitude and adjusting a little more with her new boss. Tarot also suggested that the less she fought with her boss the better it would be for her. She was advised to be more accommodating towards the new changes presented to her.

She called after a few months. She had had her promotion as against what I had predicted, but it was because she had done as advised, changed her approach to work and therefore gained a better future. If Tarot hadn't shown where she stood as on that day, she wouldn't have got the promotion and, instead, would have lost her job. Tarot thus gives you the power to change your destiny. Positive thinking and a strong belief system can go a long way in changing your life from the present state. Tarot is this source of positive energy. It shows you what you need to do to get what you desire. If your cards predict a certain future and it isn't what you want, then the solution is simple – what you are doing at present isn't working for you. Thus change your actions, increase or reduce your efforts as per your Tarot reading and get what you ultimately desire.

Most of my patrons visit me at a time or stage in their life where they have either given up on hope or feel lost and defeated by life's struggles. Besides predicting their future, my Tarot readings focus on what the future looks like depending on their present stance. I inform them about this undesirable future if so predicted or a desirable one as per the outcome of their readings. In a situation where the readings are undesirable, I gently guide them to how they can change their life, by instilling faith and courage in them that they have the power to change their destiny. Tarot guides you and shows you where you will be if you walk a certain path. If the destination is not what you wanted, change your path and transform your life.

Astrology, Numerology or any other form of occult mostly dwells on your life and tells you what is in store for you in time. Tarot goes beyond all this. It definitely tells you what is in store for you in your future and also gives you the magical power to transform your life. No one can take this power away from you and Tarot's indicative philosophy only reaffirms this. The reading that you do can reflect this change from time to time depending on how you decide to shape your life on the basis of the future predicted in your last reading. Tarot is like a guide or a mentor who holds your hands and takes you to your success. Every step that you take, every change that you bring about in your life on the basis of your Tarot readings will reflect a different and a better future. It all depends on how you use this power of Tarot to your advantage.

Tarot as a Counsellor and a Way to Spiritual Enhancement

This third and last element of Tarot is something I have mastered over the years of practice and experience, my personal contribution to enhancing Tarot readings and their potential to guide lives. Tarot doesn't necessarily play a direct role of a counsellor or guide to spirituality but it does so indirectly, through me. When I started doing Tarot, initially, it was only limited to two elements: a medium to predict the future and to change your destiny by showing you the way forward. As I grew in my experience as a Tarot card reader, I realized that most of my clients kept coming back to me to be healed and, most often, just to open up and pour out their heart to me. Most of my experiences revolved around helping clients battle their life ahead through constant motivational talks and strategies to help them create a better life. This led me to study Psychotherapy and Counselling. I did my master's while I was practising Tarot and it helped me immensely to shape my clients' lives for the better. The scientific understanding of human psychology enabled me to come up with interesting behavioural therapies, methods of psychotherapy and various ways of counselling. Sometimes I deployed assertive therapy, sometimes aggressive therapy, and sometimes plain pep-talk therapy. My intervention as a counsellor started to bring about huge positive changes in my clients' lives. They developed a more positive and healthy lifestyle and started achieving more out of themselves. This art of positive reinforcement and scientific intervention was initiated through Tarot in my life. It helped me become an expert at reading the mind and heart and guiding my clients on the basis of these enhanced readings. I struck the right chords of intuition and scientific intervention to heal my patrons. This brought about a phenomenal change in my own perspective of life and a 360 degree shift in my outlook. I started seeing things differently. This is also the time that Vipassana happened to me. Vipassana is the art of self-realization, a way to Nirvana, the method practised and preached by Gautama Buddha. This further enlightened me and opened the door to spirituality. I dedicated a lot of time to study spirituality and ways to attain self-realization through meditation. During this time I came upon various forms of meditation to heal my clients by helping them reduce stress-related problems, address interpersonal issues and guide them towards self-realization. Self-realization is an overwhelming concept or perhaps it is the perception that makes it so. Hence I will dwell a little more on its details to give you a brief understanding of what this concept truly means with respect to Tarot and how these three benefits that you derive from Tarot are interrelated through the author's note in the end.

How Is Tarot Different from Numerology and Astrology

If you have ever wondered how Tarot predictions are different from Astrology and Numerology, let us unravel this mystery now. In most cases, you would have your own preference for Astrology or Numerology. In picking up this book, you are giving Tarot a chance and I am sure you will not be disappointed.

Astrology is the study of planetary positions in relation to your birth date and time. Through this celestial study, an astrologer can predict your personality, strengths and weakness, and past and future events. In Astrology, the sun and the moon's positions play an important role in the celestial chart that reveals a person's destiny. As these planets revolve and change their positions, so does an individual's fate.

Numerology is a symbolic study of numbers and reveals one's characteristic traits. This study of an individual's characteristics helps us in understanding his strengths and weaknesses, which can then be applied to various aspects of life like work, love or health to get the best out of them. This study is done through the frequency of energy emitted by these numbers within the physical universe. The birth date plays an important role as most numerological predictions are based on it.

Tarot is a set of cards used to predict one's future. Tarot reading is not just about the cards but also about the reader's intuitive skills. Every individual possesses what we call a sixth sense, but only a few develop it to reach a point where it can become a power, beyond the understanding of normal consciousness. This intuition, when combined with the mystical Tarot cards, becomes a perfect tool to predict your destiny. Tarot is thus very different from Astrology and Numerology. It isn't scientific as the other two mediums but it is definitely metaphysical.

What is this Metaphysics? It is the branch of science or philosophical science which studies the less explicable concepts, like the existence of God, the study of what is there and what isn't, what is cause and what effect, what exists, why and how. It is the study of all reality, visible and invisible, natural and supernatural; for instance our belief in the existence of spirits whether evil or benign, or of the origin of the universe which, despite all the scientific reasoning and explanation, still retains a tiny seed of mysticism. Another such example is the belief in life on other planets; we haven't discovered this but we do believe or at least argue about the existence of aliens and UFOs. One may not have seen God or experienced divine presence, but the belief in God's existence is strong. You may even want to consider the human soul; it has no form, no colour, but we believe that it exists. In my experience, intuition too belongs to such an area of study and exploration. How can one explain the sixth sense, the intuition that something will happen or it may not, the intuition that guides me to predict your destiny which is unexplicable but with results that are acceptable and believable? This is the place where Tarot fits in perfectly. One can't explain it yet it is remarkably accurate.

Tarot predicts everything that you may want to know about your life. You just need to find the right reader. Therefore the accuracy of Tarot cards entirely depends on the skill set of the reader. A reader develops this skill with great effort by deploying techniques of meditation, patience and constant study. The knowledge of these tools makes the reader sound in her intuition, thereby helping her relate better with her deck of Tarot cards and providing a prediction that is unmistakably precise and accurate. Astrology and Numerology lack the mystical divinity which a Tarot reader brings through her intuition. The cards whisper your destiny into the reader's mind and enable forecasts for your life.

Astrology uses planetary positions and Numerology the science of numbers to foretell your future. Tarot uses a set of colourful vibrant cards. Let me explain how these cards work. All the 78 cards in the deck I use belong to one of the four universal elements: fire, water, air and earth. Fire denotes passion, water emotions, air knowledge and thought process, and earth all the worldly goods like wealth and health. Tarot comprises of Major Arcanas (major cards which predict characteristic traits and the distant future) and Minor Arcanas (minor cards which predict recent developments in one's life). Like in a normal card deck, Tarot also has four suits – wands represent fire (passion and work), cups represent water (emotions), swords represent air (the mind) and pentacles represent earth (wealth and health).

Unlike Astrology and Numerology, Tarot predictions are dynamic and are subject to change depending upon the efforts you put in to change the future. This dynamism makes Tarot magical and intriguing. Tarot is the only form of occult which gives you the power to change your destiny. My Tarot readings for your future, as detailed in this book, are based on the twelve zodiac signs, the mystical Tarot cards, and my own trained and unerring intuitive abilities. The categorized sections have been designed to make it simpler for you to relate with your future as predicted in this book. Limitation in performing individual readings has led me to this segregation which is convenient as it clearly separates you from the rest in a specific zodiac sign. Tarot is most definitely intriguing and brings in a refreshing perspective and serves more as a guideline than purely a medium to predict one's future. Besides just predicting the future, it offers solutions, warnings and guidance for what is to come. These cards, 78 in number, talk to me about your destiny. Let us find out what's in store for you in 2017.

Terms to Remember

While you read this book, you may often come across terms like querent, healer, medical practitioner, therapist, instructor, guide or mentor. These terms remain common to two aspects of life – health and spirituality. Health for obvious reasons; you will come upon a doctor, a healer or a therapist in the year ahead to deal with one or the other small or big issues related to health. The term mentor or guide may often be seen in your spiritual reading or sometimes also in your career predictions. This mentor or guide is mostly a person or an object that shows you the way to spiritual enlightenment. As I see a mentor or a guide in your cards, so these terms shall appear in your spiritual readings across the twelve volumes. The words may even appear in your career readings; this indicates a helping hand in the form of a senior, a colleague or a new entrant who may open doors to new and better opportunities. The term querent means the person who poses questions to the reader. In this case it will be you. If you find them repetitive it is simply because they form the essence of your reading.

A few other terms may also appear frequently in this book. These could be situations which occur repeatedly in your readings. There are just 78 cards in the deck and repetition is bound to occur. However, I would like to keep you informed about the implications of these situational readings:

- Wealth creation – This implies an opportunity or a possibility to generate more wealth.

- The dilemma between two opposing elements – This implies two people, two aspects or situations that will be opposite in nature and may thus create confusion or a dilemma in choosing between the two.

- A sudden revelation or the ugly truth – There are certain cards in Tarot that denote the appearance of truth which is usually hidden in the background. When this truth comes out, it brings with it devastation and traumatic change.

- Loss of wealth followed by gains – This means you may have faced some financial difficulty initially. But towards the end, positive cards indicate a positive change through a sudden gain. This instant change occurs due to your power to take control and act on the situations to bring about a favourable outcome.

- Wealth from gambling – This implies a sudden inflow of wealth that comes to you due to luck. This wealth may come from sources like gambling or lottery and doesn't imply any integrity quotient. This is plainly my way of informing you that money will reach you in one way or the other. These two could be the most probable manifestations of luck.

I hope you enjoy unravelling your future and use this information for your good. With this I leave you with your destiny in 2017. Happy reading!

AQUARIUS
THE BOOK OF STAR

Your Tarot Trump

I have known him for a very long time. He came to me the first time for the usual reason – to know the future. As he started meeting me year after year, I got to know him better. He helped his wife with her goals, then his friend to achieve his goals, and finally, he decided to extend a helping hand to society in general. So he visits me now to know what he can do for society. He most definitely has plans as all of you do, but his eagerness to help others, to reach out as soon as he can, makes me feel warmly about him. He is a sweetheart, a gentle, kind and compassionate soul. I am certain he is reading this book as you are, and like you, he may be smiling at my description of him, a typical Aquarian. You are compassionate, a visionary of sorts with the tendency to look into the future and hence you forget to live in the moment. The present time is thus characterized by eccentricity, mood swings and, of course, unpredictability. This is driven by the larger humanitarian cause that you want to achieve in the near future. I have seen my client lose friends and go through difficulties in relationships, and all because he forgets to live in the 'now' rather than in the future. But yes, since you are such a generous zodiac, a selfless person, though isolated, you manage to keep your life together as you love people and are a people's person. People love you for your intellect and knowledge. I have a name for you, the Encyclopaedia of Knowledge. And so are you – kind,

*gentle, knowledgeable, and a humanitarian with a pinch
of eccentricity and unpredictability. You are a visionary.
Your vision is for the world, not for your own self. You are
kind-hearted and compassionate.*

The card which is associated with you in Tarot also primarily depicts the future. This is the single most important link between you, the Aquarian, and your card, the Star. What a beautiful name! It almost immediately lights up your face, brings a quick gleam to it, doesn't it? As a matter of fact, that is the effect the Star card has on the querent when it appears in his/her reading. Star is in a way a very bright and happy card. You are correctly associated with this card for many reasons. I shall elaborate as we unfold your relation with the star. To begin with, let's first take a close look at your card. Look intently at the Star from the Rider Waite Tarot deck that I use. What do you see?

The card shows a nude woman at a lake. She has a pot in each hand and seems to be pouring water from one of her pots into the lake; with the other pot she waters the soil and is engrossed in the activity. The card has a blue background with stars shining above. Each star has eight points; there are seven white stars with the largest, yellow, in the centre. The woman rests her right foot in the water while her left knee rests on the ground that she waters. Behind her, you can see mountains, trees and plantation. In the real sense, this is what the card represents: the female angel represents Aquarius, you. You are the pure soul whose purpose is to maintain harmony. The woman's nudity symbolizes your innocence and oneness with creation. You do not consider yourself separate from the world or its entities. The lake represents your super consciousness. The pot from which the angel pours water into the lake denotes your spiritual acts; you pour knowledge and wisdom in your pool of super consciousness for discovery and self-growth. The pot that pours water into the soil symbolizes your acts of kindness unto others to establish harmony between two worlds, the spiritual and the material; basically, it indicates all of your humanitarian work. The seven stars denote the seven chakras – your aura. These stars have eight points each. The Star card is numbered 17; 8 in Numerology, thus the eight points of the stars in this card. Eight in Tarot stands for the Strength card, which implies inner strength to heal the world and overcome all odds.

As an Aquarius, you are the water-bearer, one who provides to others and then to the self. You have taken up this humanitarian cause of providing wisdom, kindness and love to the world. This is your link with the Star card. In Star too, the angel is the water-bearer, learning and then imparting her knowledge to the world. You are the foresighted water-bearer. The large yellow star represents a hopeful future, its light glowing and cutting through the darkness, giving the darkness a bluish gleam of hope. This is why you are future minded, a visionary. You are noble, practical and precise. You believe in tomorrow; you live in the future. You are the most hopeful zodiac sign. This is what the Star card conveys. It points to a star and denotes that if you follow this star you will reach your destination. It may neither be tomorrow, nor soon, but definitely in the future, thus making this a very future-oriented card. When this card appears in a reading, it promises hope, a possibility that your dreams and aspirations are likely to be fulfilled if you cling to hope. This is typically the aquarian style, living and loving the future. The only flaw I see in this card is its uncertainty with respect to how distant the future seems – a year, five, ten, twenty years? One can never predict. Herein lies a problem with you as Aquarius; you are eccentric, unpredictable and unreliable when it comes to emotional support. Your aloofness makes it difficult to depend on you and this drives away emotional privacy. Your friends and companions can probably have difficulty relating with you on an emotional level. You can be quite the charmer at one time and totally unpredictable the very next.

The Star card is about new ideas, creations and distant hope. You are highly creative and driven by remarkable comprehension skills which evoke brilliant concepts. This makes you an asset in your professional field. This can also be attributed to your element, air. Air represents brilliance in communication and thoughts. You are clear in your thought and excellent with creative concepts, most often abstract ones. Air is also associated with humane causes. You are cooperative and helpful by nature and try to understand the perspective of others. This makes you my star zodiac. You have a keen sense of intuition as well. Your sixth sense is strong and, if developed, can take you a long way in knowing the unknown. You must consider harnessing your intuitive skills. On a spiritual level you are very close to attaining enlightenment. Your purpose is self-realization and, unknowingly, you are already on this path. Now that you know this, I especially recommend that you focus on your spiritual self. Your Spiritual reading for 2017 followed by the chapter 'Author's Note' is a good place to start.

As Star (Aquarius) you have a lot waiting for you in the year to come. However, a lot of goodness that awaits you depends on how you cope with the people around you. We are social beings and our interactions are responsible for our successes or failures. Hence it is very important that you know how to deal with the other eleven zodiac signs, the other eleven Tarot trumps. Each one of them will respond to you differently, some favourably and some not so favourably. The next chapter delves into your compatibility quotient with the other signs. Let us have a look at it as this knowledge will help you formulate your actions better with them.

Your Tarot Compatibility

You are the Star, a person of hope. You are possibly the most optimistic sign of all zodiacs. In fact your optimism is sweeter as it is projected towards larger humanitarian causes. You live for others and put others ahead of you. This is all very good as long as you are in fields such as political or social service, but when you are involved in a life of your own, where you have family, friends, business associates and lovers, this attitude can become a problem in itself. Not all can have the same vision as you. Not everyone may be as foresighted or as selfless as you. Your intellect, your hunger for knowledge makes you one of the greatest zodiacs but it also brings with it the unpredictability and eccentricity which you so prominently display. You are a people's person but your constant longing to think beyond the normal makes you choose isolation and freedom above all. You are reckless, sometimes too independent. Thus we need to figure out who would serve as a good partner for you in all walks of life, be it in love, business, family, friendships, or at work.

In this mad world where you will interact with the other eleven signs, it is difficult to know which of the eleven will adapt to your dynamic personality and which will not. You are a very knowledgeable and lovable person who will need someone who can relate to your quest and passions equally. I have listed the Tarot trumps that will be most compatible with you, a few who are indifferent to you and a few others who make pathetic matches with you. This should help you understand and work upon the best and worst matches, the least compatible and the average. Like you, the other eleven zodiac signs are also described by a Tarot card each. Let us get to know them first before we understand your compatibility quotient with them.

Aries – The Emperor Card (fire)

Taurus – The Hierophant Card (earth)

Gemini – The Lovers Card (air)

Cancer – Chariot Card (water)

Leo – Strength Card (fire)

Virgo – The Hermit Card (earth)

Libra – The Justice Card (air)

Scorpio – The Death Card (water)

Sagittarius – The Temperance Card (fire)

Capricorn – the Devil Card (earth)

Pisces – The Moon Card (water)

Each of the twelve zodiac signs has its own trump card. Each is an ace in Tarot and has its own qualities. Keeping these astute qualities in mind, the Tarot perspective, and considering my years of experience in client reading, I can tell you that the forthcoming combination of your sign with the other zodiacs should be the most appropriate in any given situation of life. This compatibility quotient is applicable to one or all of the aspects of life (love, health, wealth, career and spirituality). This chapter will give you your best compatibility score with people you interact with in all walks of life – your spouse, boss, business partners, offspring, parents, colleagues and friends. We begin with the most compatible Tarot trump (the zodiac associated with it).

The Tarot trump which is most suitable and compatible with Star (Aquarius) is Lovers (Gemini).

Element: Star=Air=Lovers

Score: 8.5/10

Your best matches are fellow air signs. Air represents love, passion, sensitivity, intellect, talents and gifted communication skills. Air signs are also considered fun-loving people who will have large social circles and a great circle of close friends. You thus need someone who will understand these important attributes about you and tackle you accordingly. The fun-loving, creative and the very interesting Lovers (Gemini) fit the bill perfectly. They love attention as much as you do; they are easy to be with, fickle, adventurous, passionate, and full of life. These qualities of a true Lover are very endearing to you. You want someone who will not be an impediment in your quest for humanitarian causes. You will love to be with someone who appreciates freedom of space and time. You are sometimes eccentric and highly unpredictable; this is not easy to deal with. Lovers will love this fickle and unpredictable nature of Star, which so closely matches their dual nature and thus makes them a perfect match for you. They share the same hunger for intellect, eagerness to learn and know more, and are driven by passion and adventure. These qualities give you the freedom you desire, the motivation you need and the companionship that can be the perfect friendship and the best union. They love their freedom and space and dislike overbearing nature. As business associates or co-workers, this match will be like an adventurous ride full of creativity, passion and intellect. As lovers, this is a very endearing match which is focused on enjoying life to its fullest with complete ease. Within the family, this match will offer freedom to each other and perfect harmony and understanding to keep the family bond strong. Given its compatibility, this relationship scores the highest, 8.5/10.

Element: Star=Air=Justice

Score: 8/10

Another good match for the Star is the intelligent and versatile Justice (Libra). Justice is as hungry as you for knowledge, art, beauty and creativity. It is a versatile and talented zodiac. It is communicative and articulate, an impressive and intelligent zodiac. You, the Star, share these qualities with the flirtatious Justice. You are as intelligent, knowledgeable and passionate. Justice in Tarot is most known for its balance. It is the sign which can balance difficult situations or people. And this is exactly what it does in your relationship. Libra balances your eccentricity and unpredictability with its love and harmonious nature. It maintains the balance as far as it can but sometimes, with your strange need to isolate and introspect, you can push this balance off the limit and the relationship could then turn lopsided. Libra is known for its active social circle and so are you. However, Justice tends to please people and desires attention most often. You could perceive this as their weakness and this in turn could lead to resentment. Due to this small problem, I score this match an 8/10 for its compatibility with you.

The match of two similar zodiac signs and Tarot trumps, i.e., a Star with another Star is also a good one. You will know each other's strengths and weaknesses well. This will help you both cope well with each other in all aspects of life. It is like living with your mirror image. The only difficulty in this situation is the fact that too many similarities can make this relationship predictable and take the fun away. Otherwise, two similar trumps make for a very good match.

Element: Star=Air with Temperance=Fire

Score: 7.5/10

There are certain elements which will be compatible with you despite their opposite nature, an attraction difficult to rationalize. This incredible score is due to the magical alchemy of air and fire. Air is all about passion and love whereas fire is all about adventure and drive. This is a fantastic combination of opposites with so much zest and enthusiasm that it can simply be branded as the best match for Star. However, let us begin to understand these three signs in co-relation with you. Temperance (Sagittarius) is a sign of adventure, balance, futuristic goals and moderation. It is known for its attractive personality and flirtatious charm. It is a very endearing and a highly charged sign obviously because it is a fire element which is known to be dominating and authoritative. Sagittarians are also a very fearless sign; they will leap before they think and this makes them courageous and desirable to the opposite sex. The Star that you are is humanitarian and foresighted and gels really well with the carefree and adventurous Temperance. Temperance shares the same attitude towards life, foresighted and future-oriented. The only difference here is in the fact that Temperance's vision is for the self and Star's vision is for others at large. In either case, Temperance gives freedom, motivation and encouragement needed to live in the future. You and Temperance make for a cheerful, vibrant match; both are focused on a happier future and will always have big dreams. This larger than life vision keeps you together and driven. I thus score it a 7.5/10 despite fire and air's opposing nature.

The other fire sign which goes well with you is the Strength (Leo). Strength is known for its majestic aura and strong heart. As a Star you will completely enchant the Leo with your intellect and sparkle; you too will be enamoured of the pompousness and beauty that Strength brings into your life. Strength adores luxury, art and beauty and this is something that you too like. You hit it off well until Strength's penchant for the limelight gets too much for you. Similarly, your overbearing, though selfless, humanitarian work coupled with your brand of eccentricity can throw off the carefree Strength. If these differences can be resolved, this union can be a fiery combination. The Emperor (Aries) is a sign of leadership and power. The Emperor represents dominion and authority. It will give you direction and a sense of power in your relationship and will help you stay focused. However, the problem arises when you become eccentric in the pursuit of your larger goals and begin to isolate yourself. Of all the fire signs, Emperor is the most emotional one and tends to reject this behaviour immediately. Unlike your match with Temperance or Strength, this match can be a little volatile. However, Emperor could be a wild card that decides to put up with your unpredictability for the sake of your love of adventure and freedom which it so desires.

To win a battle it is always good to know your strengths, but even better to master your weaknesses. In life we come across different people who have different perspectives. Not everyone is as good a match with you as water or earth; there will be others who will be a mediocre or at times horrible. It is good to know what kind of people you meet and what kind of a compatibility score you share with them.

Element: Star=Air with Hierophant/Hermit/Devil=Earth

Score: 4/10

The element which is your total opposite, in a negative sense, is earth. Air denotes fun, thrill, fickle-mindedness, intellect and an articulate mind. Air signs are also gifted with excellent communication skills. Air signs are fun-loving and can initially have a good relationship with earth elements like Hierophant

(Taurus), Hermit (Virgo) and Devil (Capricorn). Over a period of time, you realize that your ideals don't match theirs. Earth denotes pragmatism, logic, scepticism, loyalty, security and, most of all, stability. They are homely, a little reticent, and very warm. The earth elements cannot deal with the air element's fickle and frivolous nature. They perceive this passion as nonsensical and impractical. There is no scope of greys for the earth signs. Air is all about the grey shades and very little clarity. A Star's worst match is with Hermit. Hermit's sense of perfection and meticulousness can push you off the edge. You will begin to lose interest very soon and find Hermit's interventions overbearing. On the other hand, a Hermit will not be able to tolerate your eccentricity or unpredictable nature. It is either the Hermit's way or the highway in case of a relationship. It can never be the Star's way. These differences also apply to your compatibility with Hierophant and Devil. The Hierophant is too practical and stubborn to deal with your ways and the Devil is way too dedicated and focused to watch you isolate yourself. The Devil will make you the focus of its life and seeing you isolate and behave unpredictably will erode this focus, causing it to look outside for solace. This match is highly impractical and illogical; the combination of earth and air in this sense is terrible and faulty. I thus score this match a low 4/10.

Element: Star=Air with Chariot/Death/Moon=Water

Score: 5/10

There are some who will match perfectly with you, some who will make for interesting combinations, some will not match at all, and a few others who may just be indifferent. This section of this chapter is focused on exploring such indifferent matches with you, the Star. Among all the elements, water is the most indifferent to you. Water is known to be the most powerful element when provoked but otherwise the most undermined of all. Its power lies beneath its calm but its sensitive and loving nature misleads one into believing what is seen. Water signs like Chariot (Cancer), Death (Scorpio) and Pisces (Moon) are the most driven, powerful, focused and sensitive signs. These signs represent an inner strength, a sense of calm which, when provoked, can turn into the quiet before the storm. The Star that you are tends to take these gentle, loving and sensitive water signs very lightly. You continue to be on your larger humanitarian quest, ignoring the romantic or attention-seeking needs of these elements. Water signs like Scorpio and Pisces require constant love and admiration. Well, this may not interest you in the long run and thus you may walk away with a relationship that puts you out of focus and someone else into the limelight. Of all the water signs, the Chariot alone is understanding and intelligent enough to see beyond its needs and look into your desires. This makes the relationship work but not for too long due to Cancer's heightened sense of romance and emotional needs. You are a very independent and isolated sign whereas these watery elements need constant love, attention and admiration. This relationship or association can work only when the water signs decide to put their needs in the backseat and keep you in the front. Doing so can erode them in the long run causing monotony in the relationship. I thus give this match a score of 5/10 considering its differences with you.

I am sure this knowledge of your compatibility with other signs will help you in the future. Let us now begin to unravel the mysteries of 2017. We will first take a look at Love predictions for the year and later delve into the four important aspects of life – Health, Wealth, Career and Spirituality.

Your Love Life in 2017

You are the Star in Tarot, a card that denotes lasting hope and goodness. You are a positive sign that looks into the future and believes all will be well. This is a very strong approach towards life; an optimistic attitude like yours will attract the right people and things. However, there are times when we face uncertainties. In matters of the heart, these uncertainties play a crucial role. In fact, your unpredictability and humanitarian nature may not go down too well in case of a lasting relationship. Some lovers will stay and some won't, marriages may last or may lose the spark. Let's look into your love predictions for 2017 and reduce the uncertainties.

January

The year has started and you are eager to initiate new developments and work towards achieving a certain balance in your existing love relationship. I see you starting the year on a good note where there will be happiness and love. A little further into the month and troubles begin to brew. You may be going through certain difficulties in other aspects of your life which impact you negatively and so also your love life. You may feel withdrawn and dejected and this will leave you feeling lonely. You may choose to stay with yourself in isolation for a while. Well, this is not a good sign and you should begin to focus on your love life before it gets affected. Towards the end of the month I see some positive developments. You will be clear with

15

what you want from your life this year and this clarity will clear the air in your relationship. You will once again be back in it where you will now be ready to give your best to your partner.

For the unattached Star, there is hope in love this year. You will be seeing positive developments in love if you choose to focus on it. Try and make time for love. Somewhere in middle of the month you may begin to feel depressed and sad about being lonely and isolated from those who have partners. But this sadness is only very temporary as I see you getting back into action by motivating yourself towards a brighter future.

February

There is a need to get organized and a bit more disciplined in love. If you are not giving it its due attention, then troubling times await you ahead. There will be a shocking event that will take place in your love life this month. This revelation could be a reality or a truth which was hidden for a very long time and would have finally raised its ugly head now. This truth will destroy your dream castles and sabotage your love life. You will be sad and dejected but somehow may decide to give your relationship a second chance. This chance may come in the form of a new promise or a development which will give you the courage to stay in it and work on it once again.

For the single water-bearer you may find yourself being attracted to someone much older in age. This is going to be a difficult phase where this attraction knows no limits. But do look out for a shocking truth that comes your way. This truth may throw you off the line and leave you feeling dejected and disappointed in love with this older person. Apparently you will muster courage and decide to give love a shot again by getting ready to face what comes next in life.

March

There is a strong feminine energy influencing your love life around this time. If you are a woman Aquarius, this feminine energy could be you; if not, then it will be your partner who will be in complete control of this relationship. This is good considering that I see new strategies and ways being worked upon to achieve peace and harmony in love. You will be receiving good news in terms of childbirth, something you have been working on. Besides this, marriages, engagements and happy ceremonies are on your cards. In general this is a very happy month where I see one good news following the other, especially towards the end of the month. You will be ready to take on these new developments with enthusiasm that knows no limits.

This is a good month for the single Star who will take matters of the heart very seriously and decide to work on achieving targets in love. The prospects of happy relationships are on your cards where you may be considering serious commitments, marriage or an official declaration of love. You will be eager to take your love life to the next level and trust me, there is a lot to look forward to as I see you getting ready for something big coming your way in love.

April

You are going to see some tough times this month. There will be some difficult arguments, discussions and issues which may be beyond your control. If either of you is involved in a clandestine love affair, then this may be the end of it. You will be seeing some challenging times where you and your lover will be poles apart from understanding one another's problems. However, once this phase settles down, you may begin to move towards happiness and stability. I see you doing well when you decide to put the past behind and move on. If you have been awaiting a positive news that will shape your love relationship, then chances are it may get delayed further but will eventually come.

The unattached Aquarius may go through a difficult time where you will be questioning your chance and fate in love. If you are drawn into something that may not last, it is best to stay away. Don't seek solace in something that may not have a lasting future. The mid-month once again uplifts you and gets you out of the darkness of suspicion and doubts about finding true love. I see you awaiting the possibilities in love eagerly and it is very much on its way. Just be patient.

May

You will be tempted to look outside of your committed relationship around this time. Keep that indulgent side in check and don't let that devil within get unleashed. Also do look out for being dominated by your partner and succumbing to his/her desires. Be practical and apply logic when needed. I see you in complete control of your relationship which goes to say that you may have countered the devil within successfully. This is good but unfortunately a sad news may break upon you this month end. You may come to know of a truth which your partner concealed for a very long time or may come upon a distrustful event. But I see you recovering from it quickly, which is good.

The unattached Aquarius may find it difficult to resist the temptation of falling in love with a hypnotic character. This person may not be ready for love but may be looking out for some fun and thrill. Know where you are headed before you get into it. You will fortunately decide to take control of yourself and direct your energies towards something more serious. The end of the month may bring forth disappointing news that will leave you heartbroken but the damage is temporary and you will move on soon.

June

You will be doing well in your love relationship as we start this month. I see you moving forward and making progress in achieving stability in your relationship. But there will come a time where you may be constantly facing defeats in love from your partner. Your partner may be putting you down and disregarding your efforts. This will leave you feeling hurt and angered at the same time. However, I won't recommend you to put up a fight. You will have your chance soon. Be patient. Do not feel restricted in this relationship and if you do, which I see happening, break free by speaking up. You should exercise your freedom of thought and speech. Do as you want to and not what the other desires you to. Do not feel constrained and restricted. Break free!

The single star will be meeting a knight in shining armour or Miss Perfect this month. You will be head over heels in love but this attraction may turn out to be fatal as this person has the tendency to put you down and make you feel small. This whole arrangement may not be something that you like and I see you feeling very restricted and in fact not yourself at all in it. If the arrangement doesn't work for you, it's best to let go of it.

July

This is a fantastic month in a very long time for your love life will see some incredible changes in July. I see you starting something new in general which will begin to have a positive impact on your life. This is mostly new work, business or a way to generate more wealth – the onset of wealth will have a positive influence on your love life. I see the wheels of fortune turning in your favour. You will be seeing some sudden shifts and twists in your life that will make the impossible happen. You will be standing at a phase in life where you will get that one big dream you always had. If this dream is related to your love life – like marriage, a commitment or childbirth – then trust the universe for your dreams will become reality this month.

The unattached Aquarius will witness some life changing events this month. I see you meeting the perfect man/woman who you may have been waiting for. Things will fall in place for you as I see your deepest desires related to love coming true. There will be the perfect union taking place this month where I see possibilities of marriage or engagement coming through.

August

You will reach a point in life where an important decision would have to be made in matters related to the heart. The future of your love life will depend on it and therefore make this decision wisely and carefully. Do not evaluate this decision in the light of your past and look at it as an opportunity to come. I see you taking a break for a while. This may mean a break with your lover like a short vacation or a break from your lover to think clearly. In either case this break will help you in formulating a clear action plan. The end of the month sees a new beginning. You will begin to move forward on an adventurous journey which you have never taken before. This may be a big leap for you in your love life where you may decide to take your relationship to the next level. On the whole this journey is going to be exciting and challenging at the same time.

The single water-bearer will be caught up in a situation where an important decision will have to be made. This decision will shape your love life in the future. Think clearly and calmly to arrive at the right decision.

September

I see you making progress initially in this month. You will be doing the right things and life in general would be favouring your love life. However, there are chances that arguments and discussions may not go the way you have planned for them. This will leave you feeling defeated and vengeful. But hold on, fighting is not an option. During such times avoid feeling restricted and held back. If you do feel this way, speak your mind and make yourself heard to change the situation.

If you are single then get ready to be swept off your feet by a very charming character. However, this attraction may not be something that you may enjoy. After a while you will realize the shallowness of the person and may want to break free.

October

You will be doing very well in your love life this month. I see marriage, happy ceremonies and also a home purchase on the cards this October. You will be doing fantastically well for yourself and as a lover to your partner. This will be the time when you will receive rewards for your efforts in terms of love, recognition and respect from your partner. This will lift your spirits and motivate you to do better. However, look out for feelings of desperation due to a certain financial reward being delayed. The delay may seem ceaseless and this will begin to frustrate you and thereby rub off on your relationship negatively.

The unattached Star may be ready to get married and hitched for life. You will be readying yourself for something bigger and better in love. I see you receiving rewards for your patience but your desperation will push your luck away. Love will culminate if you give it a chance and wait it out.

November

This is the time when you will have to bring about a certain change in your attitude towards love. This may mean controlling your ego, learning to accommodate others and being more patient. In general, life will throw challenges at you which may not be easy to accept and adapt to. You will have teething issues, but from where I see it, the adjustment will help you in the long run. I see you losing spark and getting bored with your present relationship. Something somewhere will be amiss. You will want to work on it but won't know how. This is the time when a woman/man enters your life and rekindles the missing spark. My only worry is that this person should not be someone outside your existing relationship to whom you seem to be attracted.

If you are looking for love then this month may urge you to bring about the necessary changes in your approach to attract love. You will have to mellow down a bit and reflect on how you conduct yourself. I see you losing heart as the going gets tough in love. But hang in there and you will see a positive development in the form of a man/woman who will enter your life towards the end of November.

December

The end of the year is here. I see a phase in your love life where you turn to a counsellor or a therapist. This counsellor could be a professional help or someone from whom you seek advice and guidance. This is a good initiative and it should help strengthen your love relationship. I see you getting ready to imbibe what you have learnt from your talk sessions into your real life. There will be a certain excitement and enthusiasm to do something new. You will be ready to work on new ideas and ways to achieve stability in love and to restore peace.

The single Star will be ready to end the year on a good note too. I see you enthusiastically waiting for certain things that can help you give a start to your love life. And as you eagerly await this I see a very articulate person stepping into your life who may be the one you seek. Well, the year has ended well with positive outcomes unfolding towards the end of 2017 for a new beginning in 2018. With this we end your love predictions and move on to your health readings for 2017.

Your Health in 2017

Health is what you make of it. It can either be your wealth or your greatest worry. In fact health is like a job, the more you work towards it, the better it gets. My forthcoming readings will take you through your health predictions for 2017 and show you what's in store. Keeping these predictions in mind, you can bring about necessary changes in your lifestyle.

January

The year has started but instead of being excited and ready with a list of resolutions which most of us do, I see you battling a confusion related to your health. You could be facing tough times when your health is at its lowest and a quick decision would have to be made. This means you introspect well, think through wisely and make a decision considering your experience and concerns. If you have doubts about your health, health practitioner or even a test result which may have come out very recently, get down to the bottom of it and weed out all your doubts. Run a scrutiny of the details, of the backgrounds and unless convinced about the certainty for a treatment or a doctor, do not go ahead with it. You will have to be cautious before you choose to take the leap. I see you losing focus and getting bored with the usual routines, treatments or patterns of health checks that you could be undergoing. You fail to see the results in spite of all your efforts and this leads to a lot of questions in your mind. You may be bored to death and looking for change.

If this is so then act on it and change what you don't like about the existing health routines. While you get busy figuring this out, beware of unscrupulous characters who may cheat you in the name of health. Stay away from such people and look out for some form of deceit, treachery or theft occurring. Now that you already know what's in store for you, take heed of the actions and turn them around before such deceit actually occurs.

February

All your health related woes will end this month. I see a sudden change that will come upon you and end all your health issues. This change is positive and assures relief. It may initially come across as something drastic and devastating, but as time goes by you will realize its true essence and positive effects. A man is part of your health scene this month. He may be a new healer, doctor, fitness instructor, etc., who will help you make a fresh start. His intervention is going to be very helpful in overcoming the health problems you were battling. I also see you initiating something new and different towards achieving better health results. This could be a therapy, treatment or simply a course in meditation that helps you calm the epicentre of all problems – your mind! The end of the month brings news which is very positive. Your test results may turn out to be negative and this will leave you feeling happy and joyful. Most of your apprehensions related to your body and mind will fizzle out with the advent of this news. You will now be ready to move ahead and bring about the necessary changes needed in shaping your health for better results.

March

You will be at your emotional best as you start this month. I see you emotionally stable, happy and blessed with a fantastic support system like a family. You will generally be feeling good and upbeat about your health. As you seem to be happy inside, it reflects positively on the outside and your body and mind reciprocate brilliantly to this positive emotional stability. But this peace is short lived as I see a certain revelation or truth rocking the foundation of your health and shattering your dream castles. You will come upon a truth about your health that was always there in the background but may have surfaced only very recently due to the turn of events. This news or event will leave you feeling dejected and sad. However, it can't get worse emotionally and physically. I see you initiating positive changes and taking small steps towards improving your health. You will work on your mind first and then move to your body. This approach will help you deal with what has come along and help you recover from these low points of life.

April

You will face a defeat in health this month. This defeat may occur in any other aspect of your life like love, wealth or career and leave you feeling angry and dejected. You may want to fight back but this may not be the time and holding on to such negative feelings of despair and loss will only attract more of it. It is therefore advised that you let go of these feelings and learn to forgive and forget. This is in your larger interest. I see you taking to intoxication, substance abuse, over eating, complacency in exercising and completely losing your disciplined self. You will simply begin to give in to your indulgent side by indulging in one or all of the above mentioned acts that can ruin all your efforts in improving your health. This is not advisable and some caution will go a long way in helping you heal. So stay away from these negative tendencies and watch how you conduct yourself. Also do not put your trust too easily in people who could fleece you and cheat you with wrong information or treatments when it comes to your health. Beware what you do and with whom you deal. Towards the end of the month I see you taking control of your health and doing everything right to fix the errors. You will decide to chalk out some new plans and ways to achieve a certain health goal and correct your approach towards your body and mind. This is good, and I hope you continue to stay focused.

May

Something somewhere may have failed to work for you and this will lead you to end this association, treatment, therapy or routine. You may have put in your best but this has failed to give the desired results. You will therefore choose to end this and move on to something new which may be more beneficial to you but choosing to let go and bring about closure is not going to be easy, especially if this association was an emotional one. It will cause you a lot of pain and emotional ordeal to end and move on. In fact I see you regretting your decision as you move further into the month. Now living in the past is not going to help. You made a decision and now you must stick to it. Brooding over what was, what could have happened is all passé. You must accept what you have chosen to do and stand by it. Move ahead in life before this guilt or regret begins to have a negative impact on your health. A disturbed mind can bring more harm than a sickness or an ailment so fix these emotional issues and move ahead in life. Let go of the baggage right away. The end of the month brings in happy news. If you have been planning a baby, this month may just be right for it and you could hear good news. Marriages, happy ceremonies, prosperity, good news about wealth are part of this month's plan which will boost your spirits and leave you happy and joyous. Your health will once again be up and going and you must work on keeping it that way.

June

This month is characterized by a lot of mental tension and upheavals. You will face some challenges in your health due to emotional issues. I see you going through a dark period and you must resort to help if all else fails. Medical intervention is advised if you feel there could be an underlying mental ailment which has gone unnoticed so far. Speak up with an open mind about your problem and get it fixed before it is too late. There will be a lot of speculations revolving around your life this time of the year. A woman could be the reason for these worries and speculations. You must do the right thing and follow your instincts. Do not throw away everything just to seek temporary thrill in life. Watch where you go and guard yourself. I see you seriously worried and reaching a point where worries and tensions cause sleepless nights. You seem to be totally taken over by these obnoxious negative thoughts that you mind is churning. This isn't reality. You should free yourself from these mind games and relax. Most of your worries are only in your head and don't exist in reality. Do not make a mountain of a mole. If you have a problem deal with it instead of worrying about it.

July

Your difficulties in health will begin to settle down as you move into this month. I see you achieving a certain amount of stability and improvement. After all the bustling problems in the last month, July seems to have started off well. However, don't hold on to the past. I still see you battling emotional issues where you are holding on to negative emotions like remorse, regret or guilt. The longer you hold on to these, the more will the same get attracted to you. You will eventually become a storehouse of past baggage. Letting go may not be easy but when you think of your overall well-being, one needs to do what is needed. You must surrender to the situation and let go once and for all. A stable mind can house a stable body. Therefore don't create any more negativity. After a lot of turmoil I see you managing to get hold of yourself this month-end. You will decide to make a fresh start and give life a second chance. On an emotional front you seem to be charged up and geared, ready to take on what life presents next.

August

You will decide to initiate a new change. This may be taking up a course in fitness, yoga classes, perhaps aerobics or simple gym workouts. You will be ready to bring about positive changes, put the past behind and get serious about working on yourself. This is also the time when a woman will play an important role in your health choices. She will be calling the shots and will make most decisions for you regarding health. I see a news coming your way. This may not be something that you are expecting but may not be bad either. How you use this news will depend entirely on you. The end of the month is a happy one where I see you conquering the odds. You may have managed to make the right use of the news and defeat all the troubles that stood in your way of success. I see you victorious and truly happy with your achievement. People in general too will look up to you for your success and you may just prove to be a fantastic case study or an inspiration to others.

September

The initial few days of this month are going to be difficult. I see you battling some challenges where your health problems may worsen, like an ongoing sickness, or turn into a serious ailment for a while. You will feel totally withdrawn and isolated; you will be left alone to recuperate and this phase may cause anxiety and apprehensions. The good news is this phase is temporary and you will get over it soon. I see you beating this ailment hands down and moving up ahead in life with a regenerated body and a supportive mind. The end of the month once again poses emotional issues. You will be stuck up with what you have and will find it hard to let go. This could be somewhere related to your finances where a certain low period in wealth causes anxiety and emotional issues. You begin to worry and act desperate, trying to take desperate measures to fix the ongoing low financial period. The best thing to do during this time is to let go and give away whatever you have. This will instantly give out a signal to the universe that you want to give more and hence it will work its way to you and bless you with wealth to share. Try giving of what you have and see the incredible results.

October

You will once again manage to defeat the health issues which you could be facing so far. I would like to add this here – your will to defeat the odds and overcome any adversity is simply commendable. I think you have a daunting spirit and this needs a cheer. Continue to fight the way you do and life will certainly surprise you. I see you victorious and successful this month. You will be at your peak in health and any wish you make shall be granted. The universe would like to do you good by rewarding your wish. From the cards that I see for you, this month in Tarot is called the month of the genie. You can close your eyes and ask for anything that you need in health and trust that it will be granted. Towards the end of the month you will initiate a beautiful journey. A journey in terms of a new class, diet, health course, treatment or even a therapy which you have never taken before. This whole journey would be adventurous and exciting. You will be eager to take it up and choose to go with the flow, irrespective of any risks that may be involved. This is a great initiative and I am certain you are going to enjoy every bit of it.

November

You will be seeing a phase this month when you will have to deal with stiff competition. This competition could emerge from any area of life like career, work or love. This phase is going to be a little challenging but also exciting. You will have to keep up with the pressure and continue doing your bit. Do not feel bogged down with the pressure; fight on. You have a very good chance to win. The wheels of fortune seem to favour you this month. You will generally be feeling better and happier. Your health will look good and most situations will be in your favour. If your health was going through difficult times then this month all of that is about to change. You may just get lucky and realize that fate is working for you. The end of the month brings the aid or help that you needed so badly. This could be help offered in terms of money, medical intervention or anything else that will help you recover. Your health will greatly benefit from this. Moreover, this help will be offered as charity without any expectation of a return. You must be grateful for it and, like I said before, the universe is doing just about everything to make you feel special and loved.

December

You will attract a healer in your life this month. This man is kind, gentle and mostly a traditional medicine specialist. He would specialize in Ayurveda or such other traditional mediums of cure and his intervention would help you greatly now. After you have done your best, now comes the time when we are almost at the end of the year where you impatiently await the rewards. You wonder why the results don't seem to be visible yet. These results, the outcome of your efforts, seem to be getting delayed ceaselessly. From what I can see, the results will come if you wait it out. So be patient; the outcome is underway. Getting restless and anxious will only increase your blood pressure. You will get the results when it's the best time for you to receive it. The last few days of the year I see you managing your health very rigorously. You will be trying various permutations and combinations in order to end the year on a good note and achieve the health goals you had set out on achieving at the start. You may be seeing some difficulties now and the best way to deal with them is to try various things to know which treatment or medicines work on you. The year ends with you doing fairly well, but you are still trying to figure new ways and means to improve your health. These improvisations will take you to the next year and I truly hope you achieve your best.

Well, with this we end your health predictions. I hope you pick up the positives, change the negatives and work towards achieving the best. Let us now move on to your Wealth in 2017.

Your Wealth in 2017

Wealth is not health but a means to attain it. When one has a sound bank balance and real assets to depend on, one sleeps peacefully at night. Wealth is the source of both happiness and, often, worries. As the Star, you are the card of hope that looks forward to constant betterment and prosperity. You thrive in life and this growth in today's world is measured through the wealth and status you hold. Let's find out your graph in wealth.

January

The year has started and I see some very bright cards for you this January. As this month opens I see you battling stiff competition for your money and wealth. This may mostly be related to your work or business which sees healthy competition from formidable opponents. Your chance to win that big account or the particular assignment which can fetch the big bucks is very high. You have all that it takes to win this competition but a pinch of self-belief can only add to your will and change your fate. Mid-month brings a fantastic turn of events. I see the wheel of fortune favouring you in a very big way. This is a very good start to the year, isn't it? You will soon begin to see money come in from unexpected sources, situations move for you and lady luck begins to favour you hugely. You will be glad to know that money makes its way to you from nowhere and in a surprisingly big way. The end of the month will bring in some more happiness and joy in terms of wealth and money. You will get lucky with some long forgotten ancestral wealth or property. You can also expect wealth from gamble or lottery which is sudden and big. I see you happy and joyous, spending quality time with your loved ones, sharing these gifts that the universe brings you generously with them. This is a fantastic start to the year and I hope to see such good times continue for you. Think positive and attract all the wealth you need.

February

A very articulate and authoritative woman is going to be part of your wealth scene this month. She is quite a character and will have a strong influence on your money. She may want to take the control away from you, which is good as long as you know where to draw a line. If you can handle this intervention to your advantage then you have struck the right chords. A little further into the month and I see you investing time, energy and money in pampering yourself for a feel good factor. You will have abundance of wealth around this time and will take a break at a retreat, indulge in expensive salon or spa treatments and do everything that money can buy. You will be seeing good times when a sudden change is going to sweep you off your feet. This change is sudden and is going to be more of an imposed one. You will see sudden changes occur in the market which will lower the rate of returns on your investments and you may even have to accept a compromise or take a back seat when it comes to your wealth now. This phase will not last for too long and may turn out to be a boon in disguise. All that you need to do is go with the flow and accept what comes gracefully and work on it.

March

Wealth-wise this month looks good. I see you receiving what you most dearly desired about wealth. If it was a certain amount of money, a dream project, a lottery, a home, a certain value in stocks and shares or otherwise will come through this month. You will get what you have been wanting for a very long time. This will set the ball rolling for you and from here onwards a new journey begins. You must use this gift prudently and cautiously. This manifestation has occurred due to your strong will to do something remarkable. Use it well. I see a very powerful and authoritative man influencing your financial decisions. He is older, wise and knowledgeable. He will have all the ideas and means to help you get to where you want to be. This is good news as you have been wanting guidance that can help you firm up your financial plans well. This person's intervention will do just that and take your wealth scene to the next big level. I see you settling and moving away from all financial insecurities and problems towards the end of this month. You will reach a stage where you will be more confident about your money and expenses. You will know that you can manage it all and this will give you a certain confidence and stability. The stormy nights are over and gone. You have fought them out bravely only to see the shore of success.

April

You will have the money but somewhere you will be stuck with feeling of inadequacy. You will begin to count every penny that you have and this will bring about feelings of lack and desperation. You will eventually get what you want but to get that a certain state of mind is needed. You will have to let go these feeling of scarcity and do away with apprehensions and insecurities. The more you hold on to these feelings the more you will get into trouble. I see your victory over these odds by the time you reach mid-month. You will achieve conquest and beat the difficulties and attain stability in wealth and especially attain a positive mind-set, which is important to attract wealth. This will bring forth feelings of happiness and joy. The end of the month brings happy times where you will manifest all that you wish for. This month is depicted in Tarot by the card of genies. In such instances you need only make a wish and that shall be granted. You will get what you want and if you haven't wished for it yet, then close your eyes and quickly make one.

May

You will have to withdraw or end your association with something that may have failed to deliver the desired outcomes in your financial plans. This may mean closure of a certain set-up or your exit from it or a situation where you withdraw from investing money in a certain investment avenue. This is a good, though difficult, decision and you will be given better opportunities in time. This decision that you would have made will bring forth feelings of apprehension and despair. You will begin to worry about your choices in wealth and this will cause you sleepless nights. One negative thought will lead to another and so on and so forth. The best way to deal with such thoughts is to eradicate them. Don't identify with the mindless negative idea your mind projects. These are just thoughts and not reality. You can beat them and move ahead in life. Gladly I see you initiating a positive development which will motivate you and keep you going. You will decide to embark on a new investment plan or an idea which has the potential to change the face of your wealth if you act quickly upon it.

June

I see you initiating something new, like a new investment plan, a certain skill or vocation which will eventually lead to more money and financial stability. You will decide to acquire new skills which will help you firm up your finances better in times to come. This may mean you unlearn and learn once again. But you have the will to learn and understand how the market works and plan your moves accordingly. This is not going to be easy. I see you battling internal shortcomings and apprehensions. You will feel restricted, held back and unwilling to do what you really want to. In such cases do not get bogged done by your apprehension, break free and move on. Do as your heart tells you to. Money wise I recommend you go slow as I see your expenses exceeding your income. You may not be able to do and buy all that you wish to. But this phase is temporary and you will get over it if you plan prudently. Towards the end of the month I see you battling between two opposites which may be causing a lot of stress – two jobs, two investment plans or two people who will be pulling you apart in different direction. You must decide to let go of the less profitable and beneficial one and keep the one that works for you. The sooner you make this decision the better it will be for you.

July

You will come upon something or someone from your past this month. This chance meeting will bring back memories and refresh your mind. You may just realize that this chance meeting has a deeper meaning as it can lead to something bigger and better this month. One of your investments may have matured and would be ready to yield returns. This investment plan was long forgotten and may have surfaced this month. While you unravel the good that has occurred so far in July, the middle of the month poses some challenges. You will be immensely over burdened with your expenses and outgoings making it impossible for you to manage your expenses. You should prioritize your expenses to bring relief and share the burden of your financial responsibility with the one on whom you can depend. This situation will change but it is critical that you fix it now before it takes a toll on you. Also, do watch your work which may be going through some difficult times. Amidst all this darkness there is good news coming your way. You will achieve victory and conquest over all your financial woes. You may decide on purchasing a vehicle and fulfilling your dream. Other aspects of your finances too will look good during this time where I see you getting back into action and overcoming all the perils.

August

You will be ready to take on a new development as you step into this month. I see you enthusiastic and excited to initiate new plans for firming up your wealth. This could indicate a new investment plan, scheme or an idea that can lead you to something big. There is news coming your way and though it may not be exactly what you have been expecting, it isn't bad news either. A lot will depend on how you use this idea. As of now I can tell you will be ready to take it in the right direction and work out a way which possibly increases your net worth. The end of the month is the most exciting part about August. I see you accomplishing your financial goals this month end. Any goal or target that you may have assigned to yourself will come through and you shall see its end. You will complete your targets, see your investments reach maturity, accomplish larger goals that can lead to big money. You will have everything you wished for in wealth this month. Well, I'll leave you with this news for a while, let it sink in and make you smile.

September

Well, the happy phase that you witnessed last month rubs off on this September too. I see you ending everything and anything that was failing to work for you. You will decide to end an association, a job or an investment plan that was simply eating up your money, time and efforts. It wasn't anything that could have lasted and you could see its near end. This is the perfect time to withdraw or end this completely only for something better to come along. Post this phase I see you energised and geared up to make a fresh start and take what comes your way positively. All these recent events have made you strong and given you the courage to go forth and excel in your work and plans. The end of the month is near and I see it bring a good news for you. You will be delighted with what is going to unfold and will be eager to take on the new opportunities and developments wholeheartedly.

October

You will be seeing good times this month. I see you accomplishing your wealth goals and achieving all those targets that you had initially set out to in the beginning of the year. You will be pleased to know that your goals will be met and their returns will soon come through. This is the result of your persistence and will power. You must continue to keep it going and stay focused in order to achieve greater heights in financial stability. Mid-month there is a bit of multitasking that you may have to deal with. I see you juggling between two different jobs which could be the source of your wealth, two people responsible to give you the money you deserve, or juggling two aspects of your life like work and personal life which may be a little taxing. This juggling at this point is critical and you cannot afford to withdraw your attention from either. You will have to multitask and work towards both these aspects. The good news is that help will soon come and relieve you from this pressure. The help comes in the form of a very creative and intelligent man who steps into your life now. He may be a financial advisor, a colleague, a person you hire or someone close enough to guide you through your problems gracefully and gently. His intervention would be rewarding as it will end most of your woes and bring you ashore to stability and security.

November

There will be a dilemma causing issues in your finances this month. You seem to be perplexed and lost as to how to deal with this ongoing problem. You should withdraw from any further investments in shares and stocks around this time. In my opinion you must go slow on investments and lie low for a while. If you are confused about investing in a certain avenue involving speculations, you must resort to a thorough investigation and scrutiny of this plan. Do not be in a hurry; instead, deploy your wisdom, skills and experience in understanding and studying this project before you go ahead with any investments. If needed, you must isolate for a while and introspect to seek answers. If you seek, you will find and the solution will come from within. You just need to be patient and be very calculated about the risks you take during this time. You will counter another problem where you suddenly begin to question your financial standing and credibility. You may not be pleased with what you have and these negative thoughts will lead to more such negative emotions. You will suddenly begin to lose interest in what you are doing and this drives away your wealth. You must hold yourself together and get going before this negativity overpowers you completely. The end of the month is going to be even more difficult where I see you putting up a fight for every penny you make. This would mean pressure, stress and tensions on your work front and also a time where you investments may take a beating due to market fluctuations.

December

The difficulties you faced last month continue to cloud your financial position in December as well. I see you confused among too many options that will take away your time and energy. You will not know which of these financial investment plans, jobs or business ideas are most prudent and beneficial in building up a sound financial base. This confusion will cause a lot of dilemma and your worries won't settle unless you take a quick decision. Any wrong choice will sabotage your finances in the future completely. So be cautious about your choices. A big change is on its way. This change will come in the form of a sudden end only to bring forth a reincarnation or a transformation. This change will end all your miseries and give you a second chance towards financial stability and betterment. You must believe in this change and go with flow. The last few days of the year are left and around this time I see you receiving a good news. This news will lift your spirits and leave you thrilled and joyous. You will end the year on a good note after all those ups and downs and constant adventures. But I believe you have learnt a lot from these highs and lows of life and now it's time you use this wisdom in shaping a better financial ground for yourself in the next year. Hope is what the whole world has and so you should continue to be hopeful and positive. This is what will change the game for you, your positive spirit, for after all, you are the water-bearer, the sign of hope for the world.

Your Career in 2017

Star, the water-bearer, is known for its creativity, innovative skills and strategies. You are an achiever at work who lives by example and work towards achieving the greater good which puts others ahead of you. You work for the betterment of society, putting aside your needs to help others achieve theirs first. This quality makes you a humanitarian, but does this help you overcome the odds you may face in your career? Do others reciprocate your efforts? Well, these external and internal factors will play a big role in shaping your career this year. With the help of my career predictions for 2017 you will know what awaits you; if you don't like what you find, you have the power to arrive at a desirable outcome through your efforts and determination.

January

You will start the year well where I see you ready to take on what life presents. But wait a minute, are you under the wrong influence or are you influencing your own work wrongly this January? If the answer to either of these questions is a Yes, then try to break free from these clutches that hold you and make you dance to their tunes. In case someone is dominating you and your work, you must speak up and end this domination. This isn't good for your career. Similarly, if you are becoming lax, complacent, over worked or underperforming, then please correct these errors before they backfire in a big way. The good news is I see you taking control of your work and moving forward while doing what could be most suitable for you. You will take charge of your work, speak up and execute the tasks assigned to you really well. This should put you in a good position at work. However, do look out for what comes next – a confusion, or let's call it a predicament, which causes stress as you have to make a choice between two opposing elements. This could mean two people like two bosses, two different jobs or two assignments which takes away a lot of your energy and time. You won't be able to handle both at a time and the sooner you make a choice the better it will be for you.

February

You will accomplish your career goals this month; you will achieve the work targets, business goals or any other ambition that you had set out for this month. Your sales targets will be in place and this will bring forth a lot of joy and happiness. I see you taking your work to the next level of perfection. You will strategize new ways and means to achieve your goals in the forthcoming months. You will be assigned certain tasks that you will spearhead. I also see the influence of a good boss or a strong mentor who will guide you well to go forth and achieve your best. Apparently when all seems to be going well, a sudden revelation will rock the foundation of your career. You may come upon a certain truth that surfaces suddenly, sabotaging your career. This truth was always there in the background but was hidden. Unfortunately, it now raises its ugly head and begins to gnaw at your ambition and success. This may mean a sudden loss of position, power or client, or even your job. You will be left disappointed and broken with this event. But from here, life can only get better. This thought should bring you solace and you must pick up the pieces and move on.

March

After all that has happened with you in the last month, moving on may seem difficult. Tarot has an important piece of advice for you through the cards that reveal your future this month. It informs you to hold on to your hope. Do not give up on your dreams and aspirations. It may seem distant or even impossible to achieve but you have the power to make this dream come true soon. You just need to believe in yourself and all of it will fall in place. Remember, you are the Star in Tarot – the card of hope. Remind yourself about this and move ahead in your career. I see a very important chance meeting occurring now. This is a person or something that comes from your past. This meeting or interaction will refresh old memories and lead you to some bright ideas. You could make something big out of it if you used this chance meeting well. I see some stress towards the end of the month in your career. You may be in a difficult position where your work is being watched. You will be under the radar and any mistake may be judged and this may sabotage your career. So be cautious about your work and don't falter in your productivity. Put your best foot forward and stay focused.

April

The troubling waters in the last month would have settled. I see you moving forward in your career – in fact not just going ahead but achieving conquest in it. You will beat the odds and come out victorious. Your work would be impeccable, making you the top performer or a game changer this month. You will be back in the game feeling victorious. You fought well and fought hard. Victory is yours in April. This leads to the end of something that was probably failing to deliver results. You may decide to pull the plug and move away from a certain department, unit or work that may not be right for you. Although you have done well, this isn't what you would like to see yourself doing. This decision would be difficult but in my opinion it is the best that you could do. Post this I see you moving forward and receiving emotionally. Certain choices can burn you entirely and you might have made one such decision to end something. But you would be doing well and moving forward in life chalking out new plans and getting ready to work on them. Emotionally I see you ready and charged to once again be back in the game.

May

You will receive good news this month. It will lift your spirits and give you a new direction to move forward. This news could come in the form of a new job opening, job offer or a change. You would be eager to try this and give this new opportunity your best shot. I see you doing very well in your work in general. Your work will be at its best where your goals, targets and deadlines would be met. You will be recognized for your contribution and people in general will look up to you for your support and advice. This will give you a high and some thrill. I see you feeling upbeat and excited about this whole victory. You will be doing well but in order to remain consistent a certain discipline needs to be maintained. You will have to get more organized and systematic in your approach and deliveries. Look back, reflect and you will know what changes need to be made to improvise. An authoritative man, a mentor like figure will enter your work scene this month. He has the authority and the charm to work his way through and could be a huge help to you in boosting your career prospects.

June

You will be standing at a juncture in your life where your career will be ready to take a new turn. I see you eagerly awaiting to initiate this new beginning which seems exciting and promising. However, in order to move on, one needs to let go. You must focus your energies on learning from the past instead of living in it. Learn to let go of your vanity, ego, regrets and failures and taking up the new prospect will become more exciting and thrilling. If you have doubts about taking up the new job or the opening, you must move on. Unfortunately, I see you battling stiff times this month where your work suddenly dips and you begin to feel isolated and withdrawn. You may be awaiting a certain bonus or incentive in the form of money which may have been withdrawn at the last minute. This will sadden you and leave you feeling disappointed. You had pinned your hopes on the incentive, bonus or salary hike; when it fails to arrive, it sabotages your dreams. This phase is going to be challenging, especially when everybody around you may be doing really well and may have been rewarded their share of bonuses. But don't lose heart, stay focused and you will see how time unfolds for you.

July

You will decide to move away or end an association or work which isn't promising. You will have to let go of this in order to follow your heart. This may mean relocation or taking up a passion by giving up something that is steady and stable. There will be risks involved but you will choose to do what your heart tells you to. This period is going to be challenging as I see you facing emotional turbulence that will make it difficult for you to stick to this decision. The card that I see for you now denotes hope and goodness. You must do as you want to and overlook the risks involved. You will eventually do well and sail through the minor hiccups which you presume to be big road blocks. You are meant to achieve greatness and unless you take this risk and make some difficult decisions you will not succeed. The end of the month brings back old memories and leads to new ideas. You will meet someone or something from the past that will greatly impact your present. This acquaintance will lead to something big if you stay focused and nurture this chance meeting.

August

You will be moving forward in your career by initiating new ways and means to achieve the most from your potential. Your career in general will be on an upward curve. However, you will suddenly develop feelings of constraint and prohibition. You will want to do new things, propose new concepts, bring about a change and speak up. But something somewhere will hold you back from doing this. It is mostly your own restricted, insecure self that holds you back from using your full potential. If you feel that the external factors are responsible for this then it is best you break free and speak up. It is about time you freed yourself from these restrictive tendencies. The end of the month brings some respite in the form of a good news. You will hear of a positive outcome that will give you another window of opportunity. You will be eager to work on it and move forward. I see you emotionally charged and ready to take up what comes next.

September

You will start this month well where the new opening or opportunity from last month will leave you excited and thrilled. You will be eagerly waiting to take up the new initiative and carve your way into the new stream of opportunities. But a little further into the month and I see you stuck up with money issues. You will face a situation where money from work may seem scarce. Your business will go through a tight phase where money flow will be scanty and expenses will be more. You will have to count every penny that you give out and this is going to cause feelings of lack and desperation. I see you holding on to your scarce means, finding it difficult to let go of it. You will dawn the role of a miser and be very selective about your expenditure. An attitude of lack will attract more lack and scarcity. I think you should reconsider your whole approach during this time. The end of the month is an extension of lack and scarce means. You will be going through an all-time low phase where money, attention and recognition will move a mile away from you. You will be left feeling isolated and withdrawn while others may have all that they need to feel abundant and happy. The positive aspect of this whole phase is the fact that it is not long-lasting and your good times will come soon.

October

You will be clear with what needs to be done next and would be looking out for an opportunity to come your way. From where I see it, you are eagerly awaiting an opportunity or a job offer from overseas which would be promising and fulfilling. Your wait will be over as I see this offer coming through. It may be a temporary shift to another country or something that could work for a short-term basis. With this new development you will be offered a better pay packet, higher remuneration and the future that promises greater financial security will obviously thrill you to the core. This offer is all that you needed but then suddenly there appears a period of confusion and darkness. You will have to rely on your intuition to guide you through it. There will be a sudden turn of events where you would begin to doubt this new offer or the people's intentions who have made this to you. Your instincts may be suggesting you to go slow and take every step cautiously while you move into an unknown territory. You must listen to this voice and follow your gut feel. If there is anything at all that seems suspicious, get to the bottom of it before you have finally taken a leap into the unknown.

November

You will have to watch the balance in your life during this time. Please do take a look at how you are balancing your personal life, health and work. If it seems to be lopsided then get the balance in place. Work towards achieving harmony and restore the missing balance in your personal life while you still stay focused in your career. I see a change coming your way. This change may not be great but it is a change that could be imposed upon you. You may have to take a backseat or even compromise for a bit while you accept this change. Very little flexibility would be offered and therefore you will have to adapt to this change. I see that you will have initial teething issues but as time goes by you will see the positives of this forced change. All that you need to do now is walk the tight rope for a while and keep moving forward. Like I said, you shall see the rewards and even before this month ends you will see the wheel of fortune turn in your favour. Situations will begin to move for you and you will see your luck change. Besides opportunities and money, your career too will witness a sea change by the end of November.

December

You will start this month well. I see you initiating a new set-up or a small venture with the intention to generate more wealth. This is also the phase where unexpected sums of money will make its way to you. You will be rather excited and seem happy with these positive developments. However, look out for feelings of boredom and lack of motivation. These negative feelings may throw you off balance and create issues in your work and productivity. You will want to change this and find motivation but won't know how to. A sudden thick fog of doubts may overtake your vision and leave you feeling troubled and distressed. But the end of the year is so marvellous and surprising that I am sure you are going to end your career predictions with a smile. I see all your dreams related to your career being manifested and become reality. If you desired a perfect job, a big assignment, an even bigger account or a particular break, it will become a reality. Whatever was on your mind regarding your career will come true this month end. I think this is the perfect end to your career predictions.

All's well that ends well. The year has ended with some positive possibilities and breakthroughs. I only hope you make the most of this and create a brilliant career. Now we move on to the next and the last aspect of life, Spirituality, which I am sure is a topic close to your heart.

The Spiritual You in 2017

Spirituality is a topic very close to my heart. This chapter has been created with the intention to give you a perspective of how your year will look if you choose to focus on your spiritual side. This spiritual side, in my opinion, is a beginning to awaken your soul. How many of us go beyond this body? How many of us even go beyond the mind? Well, spirituality is this realm which goes beyond the body and the mind. It goes to that point of your existence that connects you directly with the universe. And this point that connects your body or your mind or you with this larger universe is called the soul. Soul is called atma in Hindi, ever powerful, immortal, the greatest creation of the divine entity. It is the single most important aspect which connects you to this large universe. How else is it possible that after death, people who are reborn remember events of the past life or let's call it past births? It is simply because your soul travels through time, through spaces, through you in the various forms that you take birth after birth; through all this, your Atma (soul) remains the same. The ultimate purpose of this soul is to come into the oneness of the universe; this oneness can be achieved through realization, also called nirvana. When the Buddha attained enlightenment, he didn't become a god or a magician, he simply became a man who, through the scientific concept of meditation, achieved mindfulness. Mindfulness means awareness of the present moment. When one attains total awareness s/he becomes free from moha (desire), the root cause of suffering and pain, unhappiness and sadness. We all wish to be happy. You picked this book with the intention to know if your year ahead could be a happier one from the last. Well, this is where the buck stops. Look into your spiritual realm and you will begin to discover that happiness lies within and not without.

For now, I give you your Spiritual predictions for 2017 and thereafter, in the final chapter of this book, I have a very interesting note on how this awareness can change your life. I call this chapter the USP of my book. This is a very special chapter which holds an edge above others because it speaks to your soul. We are often trapped in the superficial aspects of our life – wealth, career, power, security, etc. Spirituality goes amiss in this crowd. This is my attempt to connect you with your soul and to show you your spiritual side and your true potential. Spirituality is natural to every being but because we are so busy being humans, we never look at the more important aspect of our life, i.e., Spirituality. This reading of the four quarters of 2017 will take you through your spiritual achievements and help you explore the path less taken.

For the Star that you are, your whole existence revolves around achieving the larger cause. You are driven by a noble humanitarian cause, a cause that requires you to connect with the voice within, the soul within. Unless you awaken the dormant soul, you will not achieve the desired success for the greater good that you are out to accomplish. The best way to do this is by creating some time and space for spirituality in your life. Up next we take a look at what you can achieve if you choose to pay attention to this path in 2017. Besides peace, you will accomplish greater feats with ease but first we begin with how you initiate your journey on this unknown path.

January-February-March

As we enter January, you would reach a stage where you could be mending a broken heart. This disappointment may emerge from any of the aspects of your life like love, wealth, health or career. You would have taken a big blow and would be seeking answers to why such an event could happen unto you, leaving you feeling dejected and disappointed. Well, this is the best time to initiate a spiritual journey. As humans, we only turn to our inner self during times of distress and pain. So while you begin your association with spirituality on not too good a note, this may be the perfect start. I see you eager to mend your broken heart, and spiritually, while you turn to yourself for answers you may realize that most of the negative events hamper you due to your personal attachment to them. However, this understanding will be at a very nascent stage and it is too early to interpret it correctly. So I see you taking control of the situation and beginning work on your spiritual discovery. You may decide to start with strategizing and planning your life in a better way to make time for this new initiative. You will begin to research and study this subject more often and may decide to give it some time to understand the concepts better. I also see the entry of a very strong and well-informed person who will help you formulate you plans better. He may guide you as to how to go about doing things in the right fashion. There's a saying, 'The teacher appears when the student is ready'. Well, in my opinion you are now ready to embark on this journey and with this new mentor it will be simpler and more rewarding. With these positive developments your life will begin to heal. I see you making a stark recovery from your earlier problems. By the time we reach March, you will be far better from where you were at the beginning; the credit for this progress would have to be given to your recent spiritual learnings. You will begin to imbibe them in your daily life and these learnings will give you the courage to face what comes in a positive way without developing attachments to it. Your recovery has begun and from here on there is no looking back.

April-May-June

You will initiate a new start this month. This new beginning is a sort of a partnership that you may enter with something or someone that is short-lived and offers great learning and understanding about the subject of spirituality. This arrangement that you may get into would be short lived and will help you form a very clear and distinctive idea about where you are headed and what to expect from this venture. You will be happy and thrilled about the new discoveries as life begins to reward you once this learning reflects in your real life. Limiting your understanding to your thoughts doesn't help; you need to cultivate the knowledge in your everyday life. You will begin this process slowly and gradually. A little further into this quarter and you may decide to take a short break and stir your mind clear from all the worldly temptations, troubles and problems. You will take a break to sit back and reflect on what life has to offer, why certain things happen to you and not to others. You will begin to search the real meaning of life. Well, this is not possible in a bustling environment, one needs to take time off, take a break in the form of a retreat to sit back and reflect on life. You may decide to do just that. You will take a short break to join a meditational retreat, or a traditional retreat which offers you some time alone to be with yourself. If you want to, you could try the ten day Vipassana course which is responsible for the huge transformation in my life. You might discover something new too. On your return, in June, I see a new you. You would have transformed not in a big way, but in a way that will open your third eye. In Hinduism, the third eye is the eye of enlightenment. You shall now know the true purpose of your life and how one can go about achieving it. You will be eager and enthusiastically waiting to take on these new developments and work on them. I see the eagerness and the readiness to do more, learn more and live a stress-free life. This is getting better by the month. Let's read on to find out how the next half of the year looks for you.

July-August-September

You will meet a very intelligent and articulate man this July who could be of use to you. His ideologies and theories will be in sync with yours and I see you two hitting it off really well. You will exchange ideas and knowledge and this man will perhaps guide you with his greater level of studies and research. You will be largely benefitted and his intervention could clear a lot of your doubts regarding the subject of spirituality. I see a very positive time unfolding in your life this August. You will find happiness, prosperity, a sound family life unfolding now. This will be simply great as I see you move closer to your larger goal – eternal happiness. You will begin to realize that happiness is a state of mind and not something that comes from external achievements. You can be happy with a single slice of bread or be sad with a feast spread out before you. It is truly a state of mind. As this understanding dawns upon you, you will begin to experience more joy and peace in your life. There will be sudden changes which you know will be in your control and sometime sadness which you will be equipped to deal with. The last month of this quarter brings a blast from the past. You will meet someone or come upon a certain thing from your past that will open a doorway to a better learning. This chance meeting is not a coincidence but a manifestation of your desires. You will definitely find something beneficial coming out of this which could lead you to smoothing bigger in your quest of spirituality. You must make complete use of this chance acquaintance and understand what life wants you to take from it.

October-November-December

You will be facing a lot of pressure, especially from your career, as you step into October. Situations may begin to get out of control and you will find it hard to cope with the pressures of the material world. You will be torn between what needs to be done and what needs to be left alone. While you could be battling these problems courageously, one way to deal with them is to surrender and accept what comes by. This way you will calm down and look at them positively. This approach may just help you deal better with stress from your career. Towards November you begin to move forward in your spiritual quest. You would have sailed through the difficulties of your career and emerged as a winner with rewards flowing in. You will suddenly strike gold. But do not get carried away with the goodness or identify with these positive outcomes so much that they negate your spiritual essence. Remember, you are developing the concept of nonattachment, the ley to liberation. So stay neutral and be calm about your recent achievements. This way happiness, success and victory will continue to grace you. Attachments can cause fears and apprehensions of loss and therefore stay detached. The last month of the year is here and this is the time when a woman teacher or mentor will enter your life. She will be a learned individual who has the gift to see through people and she will know what you need most now and what kind of teaching will help you further. She will gently but firmly guide you into the spiritual realms and this probably could be the greatest gift of the year while we are bidding adieu to 2017 and starting on a new year. I hope you continue with your quest and stay focused. As and when you need help, your teacher or guru will appear in one way or the other. All that you need to do is believe and stay detached from the material possessions of life.

Your Tarot Spreads for 2017

A Tarot spread is a cluster of cards which gives the Tarot reader a quick glance into an ongoing situation in the querent's life through the formulation of three or more cards. Tarot spreads were created with the intention to give the reader a sneak peek into problems, their causes and possible solutions. This enabled a reader to avoid series of readings; she could merely spread a certain number of cards, each depicting a certain aspect as predetermined by the reader that could help her/him interpret the querent's problems more comprehensively and quickly. There are many spreads which are ancient, some which are independently created by the reader and some which have been popularly used. Unlike last year, in this book of 2017, I have used three spreads – Celtic Cross, which is an ancient spread, Health Spread and Career Spread – which are popularly used and to an extent have my derivatives in their presentation here. These three spreads are unique and interesting for their implications in Tarot. Each of them has the following implications in a reading.

Celtic Cross Spread

This is the oldest of the spreads. Most commonly found in Tarot books, online Tarot forums, etc., it is one of the most difficult to interpret. Its objective is to find out the problem and its solution. Celtic Cross is a spread of ten cards which reveals a particular problem presently most pressing on the querent and aims at finding out its roots, causes, foundation, immediate effects (positive/negative), factors influencing it, which may or may not be in your control, and, finally, the outcome. One look at this spread and I will know what has been bothering you of late and I can, through this knowledge, help you deal with this problem in the most constructive fashion. It's a cluster of ten cards placed in the shape of a horizontal cross and each of the ten positions represents a certain aspect or situation of your life. I have mentioned the card that appeared for the particular aspect and its implications on your life in 2017

Card 1: The Present - Knight of Swords

You are at a point in your life where you are making progress and exploring new avenues. You could be involved in extensive air travel which takes you to different places and helps you network and expand your contacts

Card 2: The Challenge (the problem you are currently posed with) - World

You want to achieve everything too quickly. You have set big targets to yourself and want to achieve this immediately. But somewhere these targets are taking up your time and energy.

Card 3: The Distant Past (the foundation of the problem which gave birth to it) - Four of Cups

You had lost interest in whatever you were involved in in the past and this has led to your recent new initiatives. The need to rekindle your interest and do something new and exciting has brought you to this stage in life where you are working on a new development.

Card 4: Recent Past (the outcome of the problem in the form of its adverse effects in the recent past) - Nine of Cups

You are very excited and happy about what you have set out to achieve. This is a fulfilling emotion that gives you a certain calmness and strength to go on and follow your dream. You are convinced that you are made to achieve this big goal that you have set for yourself.

Card 5: The Recent Future (what lies ahead within few weeks or months with respect to the challenges) - Hierophant

You will meet a very important and influential man who will help you shape up your work or your passion. You must incorporate his valuable advice.

Card 6: The Outcome (which the querent desires) - Ace of Pentacles

You desire to see wealth and money flow. This is the big objective behind everything.

Card 7: Internal Factors (that are well within the power of the querent that he/she can use to overcome the problem) - Strength

You have a very strong heart that can withstand anything and a daunting spirit to accomplish what you want. You are a strong person who can achieve the impossible. You can also easily adapt and recover from low phases quickly due to these strengths.

Card 8: External Factors (that are beyond the querent's control that impact the outcome) – Three of Cups

You are looking out to complete a partnership or an association where three people are needed. But this seems to be an impossible task.

Card 9: Hopes or Fears – Knight of Cups

You are hoping to make progress and move up the ladder soon. This ambition motivates you to keep going ahead in life.

Card 10: The Final Outcome (what will eventually unfold with respect to the prevalent problem) – Queen of Swords

I see you strike a new idea, a thought that can become something really big if you work upon it. Timing would be crucial. I suggest you act fast as and when a brilliant thought comes to you. A woman too will play a critical role in your life at this juncture. Her role would be indispensable.

Health Spread

This is a seven-card spread which gives you a complete overview about your health in the present, past and for the future. The cards depict the following about your health in and around 2017:

Card 1: Present Condition - King of Swords

You would have cracked a big idea and this could change the condition of your health. You need only work on it. Your health is also characterized by a situation where a very important healer, doctor or therapist plays an important role.

Card 2: What Causes (the present health condition) - Two of Wands

Your desire to achieve a new health goal has led you to where you are today. You have made up your mind about what needs to be done next to achieve the best from your health.

Card 3: Effects (of the health condition) - Nine of Cups

You will be very happy with how you have performed so far and these new developments only bring about an emotional satisfaction and happiness.

Card 4: Corrective Measures (to be taken to fix the problem) - Four of Cups

You need to fight the tendency of complacency and boredom which usually holds you back from achieving your best. You want to rekindle the interest in such situations but don't know how.

Card 5: Challenges (opposing corrective measures) – King of Cups

You are a very sensitive and emotional person who often puts the needs of others ahead of you. You will have to be a little more selfish here to achieve what you desire from your health. You will have to put yourself first in the list of your priorities.

Card 6: Your Strength (to overcome the ailment) – King of Wands

You are a strategist and an excellent executor. You can do what you set out to very well. You can take any task to its completion and achieve the desired outcome. You are best at your job.

Card 7: Final Outcome – Justice

I see you achieve perfect balance in your health towards the end of the year where there will be perfect balance in what you eat, how much you sleep, work out, pray, etc. You will be maintaining your health well and the results will be fantastic towards the end of 2017.

Career Spread

This is a seven-card spread in a circular or an octagonal shape that delves into your Professional life. It gives you an overview of the circumstances that favour you and go against you in achieving your career goals.

Card 1: Present Situation - Seven of Cups

You are at a stage in your career where confusion is creating havoc. You have too many things to do but do not know what to choose and what to let go. You will have to think wisely and make the right decision as the fate of your career depends on this choice.

Card 2: Your Strength/Talents - Two of Pentacles

You are a juggler, one who is very good at multitasking. You can do two things at a time with perfect ease and this will help you in a big way in your career.

Card 3: Your Weaknesses/Drawbacks - Page of Cups

You are a very emotional person who would first want to connect with someone emotionally, rather than professionally for better results. But this may be your drawback as people who don't connect emotionally with you could still be right for your work.

Card 4: Factors (working against you) - Temperance

You are permuting two opposing elements which fail to

synergise. These two elements have to be combined in order to achieve a successful venture. You may find it difficult to do this.

Card 5: Favourable Factors (working for you) – Knight of Wands

You are a go-getter who loves to be on the move and initiate new things that can keep your work on top of the chart and exciting.

Card 6: Action (to be taken) – Three of Cups

You are looking to strike some kind of a partnership where three people are involved. But this is not going to be easy. Finding the three aces is going to be a challenge

Card 7: Final Outcome – Hermit

I see you introspecting deeply about what needs to be done next in your career. You may have come upon a road block which needs a quick solution. It is best to take a break from everything and think through clearly and calmly about what needs to be done next.

Author's Note

This is by far the only part of the book that explains the importance of living in the moment, i.e., in the present and does not discuss anything to do with the future. You may think I am contradicting what I practise, which in a way is true because professionally I predict the future but personally, I practise living in the moment. I do this because through my long-drawn experience I have come to understand how the concept of living in the moment, better known as mindfulness, can liberate you from all of your dukkha (suffering). In *Tarot Predictions 2016*, I emphasized the importance of this present-moment awareness. I wrote about how a complete surrender to the present can heal you, empower you and bring forth happiness. In this edition of my work I still maintain the importance one derives from mindfulness, but I would like to talk about two important aspects which can probably motivate you in practising present-moment awareness. Reading is one thing but living it is another. So through this chapter my intention is to motivate you, lure you to develop awareness – that of the present, the now, of this very moment that you are reading this particular chapter. Our whole existence as humans is based on this concept of awareness. When you are fully living in the present moment, you are free from the clutches of the past and the apprehensions of the future. These two tenses, the past and the future, do not infiltrate your life with more suffering. You are free, like the bird you see in the sky that flies without worrying about shelter, home, food or water. Flying is what it does best and its entire existence revolves around flying freely with the wind. Have you ever seen a bird trying to secure a mortgage from a bank to buy shelter, or stock food in the refrigerator for the winters or worry about who is going to hunt it down the next minute? No! The bird simply flies; it spreads its wings, gets on with what is happening right now without the slightest worry of tomorrow or regrets of the past.

We term ourselves as the most intelligent of all creations. We take pride in our superficial intelligence. But why do I call our intelligence superficial? We have created every bit of the technology to help us become more comfortable, modernize and evolved. However, does this make one truly happy? We are being dishonest about this artificial and superficial intelligence that we define ourselves with. If you are not convinced about this then let me ask you a question that will probably simplify your belief in the above statement:

Answer this – Are you truly happy now?

Take a moment and close your eyes before you answer this question. After a moment's pause, tell me, what do you see?

- Do you see the apprehensions of tomorrow which led you to buy this book?
- Do you see the horrifying past that you can't deal with and are running away from?
- Do you see happy moments you once had and the sadness that prevails around you now?
- Do you feel a longing for true love, wealth, money, a certain goal which is unaccomplished that continues to burden you?

If your answer to one or all of the above is Yes, then you must read what comes next. My dear friend, my answer to the above one or all is also a yes. I am no exception to the dukkha (suffering) that hounds us. Each of us is a slave of the past or the future. But I have come to realize a certain way to eradicate this mindlessness and free myself from the dynamics of dukkha. A life without attachment is what I am trying to emphasize; a life without desire is what leads to salvation, liberation and eternal everlasting happiness. But how on earth can two simple individuals like you and me even attain this? Good question!

I can help you formulate an action plan for your life starting now that will lead to enlightenment at least on the mental level. By that I mean the conscious level, not spiritual. Spiritual enlightenment can only come through practise and perfection in how one understands nirvana. This is a topic for another day when both you and I are more evolved in our understanding of nirvana. Today we shall focus only on achieving mindfulness in this present mad world.

I have broken down this chapter into five important parts to help you achieve mindfulness – present-moment awareness:

I. Why Be Mindful

II. How Do We Attain Mindfulness

III. Understanding Impermanence (Anicca)

IV. Understanding Aimlessness (Apranahita)

V. Mindfulness Training

Why Be Mindful

Before we discuss why we should be mindful, I'll delve a bit into what mindfulness is. It is nothing but simple awareness of the moment. Whatever you are doing right now, if you are completely aware of your actions, involved completely in the act, a total concentrated absorption of what you are doing, without your mind wandering away every second into a new thought, then you are being mindful. But 99.99 per cent of us are mindless for about 99.99 per cent of the time. We are slaves of our ever evolving, the so-called intelligent mind. It's like we have created missiles but have no time to speak with our neighbours. We have created coffee shops but we barely have the time to enjoy the coffee peacefully and silently. Our intelligent mind makes us do every bit of the intellectual thinking so brilliantly that we have accepted this is what our life is all about – creation, destruction and recreation. This is all we do and waste our time. How many of us have actually ever sat with our morning tea doing nothing but drinking it mindfully, absorbed in every sip, smelling the aroma of the tea, feeling the tinkling taste of the aromatic tea on our tongue, feeling its warmth go down our throat, travel through our food pipe into the stomach? How aware are we about drinking our tea? Well, I am sure we are not at all aware about drinking the tea mindfully. What we instead do while drinking the tea is multitask – pick up the paper, be involved in a heated discussion, haphazardly complete the chores while sipping on this freshness and, most importantly, if none of this work then think about what our mind wants to make us think like apprehensions of tomorrow, the next moment or even issues of the past. The moment we are mindful of doing the things that we are involved in (i.e. with complete awareness), we have attained freedom for that moment from our suffering. All that you need to do is to learn to harness mindfulness and apply it to every simple or difficult act in your life. The act may range from drinking tea to creating bridges, from eating your simple dinner to developing a new business concept. When you are here, in the moment and not anywhere else then you have attained the power of now. You are free from the clutches of your mind which only runs ceaselessly from one thought to the other. When you are doing something mindfully, you are completely involved in the action; there is no room for doubt, sadness or worry. You are simply here in the now, enjoying every bit of the work to be carried out. If a moment of mindfulness can give you so much pleasure and take away your sadness, then can you imagine what an hour of mindfulness could do? It can liberate you from all your worries and end your miseries.

How Do We Attain Mindfulness

Mindfulness can be developed by practising present-moment awareness. All that you need to do is remind yourself to be where you are. This practice can be applied to your walks, conversations, work, hobby, etc. Do whatever you are doing without letting your mind escape into its own world of thoughts. Do not wander away with your mind's ceaseless thinking. The moment you realize you are not here but somewhere else, bring back your attention to the act you are involved in. Do this repeatedly, constantly and gently. Do not be harsh on yourself and do not lose patience if you see yourself wandering too often. Treat your mind like a baby – it knows nothing except to playfully wander away. You are its teacher and you need to gracefully and gently bring it back to where you want it. Initially I thought that the best way to do this was to renounce everything and lead a monastic life, absorbed in meditation. Yes, meditation is the best way to train one's mind, but for a householder such renunciation is out of the question. Therefore it's best to synergize mindfulness in your daily life. My favourite author and Buddhist teacher Thich Nhat Hanh says a 'simple act of dishwashing too can liberate you'. And it truly can if you are involved in every bit of its actions starting from feeling the water, the soap, the hardness of the dishes, cleaning the vessels gently, rinsing them under the cold gushing water and putting them back in their place. A simple act of walking can be done mindfully too. Take every step mindfully – know it's your right leg that's up and left down, now it's the left leg up and right down. Feel the ground, the fresh air, the panting of the breath and know you are here in the now. Mindfulness can be practised anywhere, anytime. For modern people who are always on the phone, be there and nowhere else; when making a presentation be there and nowhere else. Do not worry about what others will think of your presentation, how your boss will react, whether you will be promoted after the presentation, etc. Just be involved fully, mindfully. This is how one can attain mindfulness in our daily lives. Everytime your mind wanders away with the thinker, let the observer in you bring it back gently to the present moment. Everytime you drift away with a thought, let the observer in you bring it back to where you should be. Initially this will be difficult as you will see your mind running ceaselessly into mindless thoughts. But laugh at its antics and come back to where you should be, in the present. When you are with your child, love the child completely and be with him/her fully. Do not let the worries of the past or the future infiltrate this moment. Keep your mind fixed on how the child responds to your speech, your love, caress and affection. Enjoy every bit of present moment awareness and your mind will gradually be tamed. Mindfulness can be attained in every second of the twenty-four hours of the day. You can start right now while you are reading this book!

ANICCA (Impermanence)

Buddhists have three important doctrines and 'Impermanence' is the first. It is also called Anicca in Pali language used during Buddha's time. I only discuss this first doctrine impermanence as this is the most important doctrine and the easiest to understand. Also understanding Anicca can lead to instant mindfulness. Thus mindfulness and impermanence are interrelated.

According to Buddhism everything in life is impermanent. I am a practising Buddhist and have realized the true essence of Anicca over a period of time. Everything starting from a speck of life to where we are, what we are going through, what we feel, what we do, what is, was and will be, is temporary. Nothing is permanent in nature. If you apply this logic to your life then you may come to understand that all of your sadness that you are going through at this very moment is impermanent, bound to change. Similarly your joys, happiness, profits and gains too are impermanent. Nothing stays forever or lasts till eternity. Nothing in this cosmos is permanent, not even our universe. Everything is ever evolving, it is dynamic. There is a constant change. What is good today may be bad tomorrow. What is beautiful today will be ugly later. What is right now would be wrong in the future. According to Buddhist philosophy nothing is permanent. This is also what Siddhartha Gautama Buddha taught. His teachings were based on the premise of impermanence. Any attachment to your existence or existing circumstances will lead to suffering. Freedom from suffering is nirvana (extinction of all concepts, ideas and sufferings). To attain liberation one must understand that impermanence is the essence of life and therefore any attachment to the present existence is foolish or insensible. The present existence could be made of sadness, joys, happiness, pain or misery. One must know that what is now will soon end for something else to arise. The moment this realization dawns upon you, you will attain true liberation. You will understand that worrying about your money is pointless. You may realize that worrying about your weaknesses is pointless – it is there today but you will certainly overcome them tomorrow. You will realize that the sadness that prevails today is temporary and will dissolve tomorrow. If nothing is permanent what is the point in attaching ourselves to maya or desire. Desire itself is impermanent. Today you desire one thing, tomorrow another and later something else. Then why waste your life trying to achieve one desire after another? Doing so will only throw you into the vicious circle of moha-maya (desires). The moment you realize this truth of impermanence, that what is will not be tomorrow, you will be free from your suffering, attachment ceases. For eg., dictatorship was impermanent, so is democracy. We have seen some of the largest countries go through these two phases of impermanence. Your human form is young today and will be old tomorrow. Your body exists today but will not in the future. Youth and beauty both are impermanent. There are umpteen examples that I can give you to help you realize this larger truth. All that you need to do is look around and you will know what I am taking about. Everything that you see comes with an expiry date as it is all impermanent. So if everything is so unstable in nature, does one truly need to be attached to them? Won't attachment to this unstable nature of situations cause pain and suffering? Thus from now on whatever phase of life you are in, know that it is impermanent. This may sound like good news or bad but again, the nature of this news too is impermanent. Do not try to fight it or secure it forever. Nothing will stay forever. The only way out is harnessing present-moment awareness where you are neither living in the past nor the future, where the worries of tomorrow or gains, profits or wealth of the now don't influence you to stay desiring this forever. The best way to deal with impermanence is to live in the moment, in the present. Unlock the nature of Being in you. Right now you are just living a human life, not that of a being. Being means ongoing, in the moment. It is time you woke up from the deep sleep of mindlessly chasing superficial aspects of life and causing yourself more pain and misery. One of the very important ways to overcome dukkha and understand the true essence of Anicca is Apranahita (Aimlessness).

Apranahita (Aimlessness)

Apranahita literally means 'to place nothing in front' and is used to designate someone who has no aims for the future. This is the definition of Apranahita from Wikipedia. This word originates from Theravada Buddhism and has profound value in the whole concept of enlightenment and spiritual realization. It is the first step towards detachment and the very first lesson taught while on your path to spiritual enlightenment. Today we all have aims and goals. Both these words mean the same. We have goals set to achieve a certain amount of money, to buy a certain home or car. We have a goal for our business, our family and we also aim to be happy wherein happiness means achieving one or all of the above. Some have goals to find everlasting love, some aim to be the best entrepreneur, some writers, actors, lovers, etc. There is no end to this whole concept of aim. Once we achieve one aim, we move on to another. It is as if the whole concept of aims and goals is ceaseless. It goes on and on. We get some kind of an adrenaline rush in seeing our goals fulfilled and then immediately we have another one. So the chase goes on and on and on. Have you ever been aimless? Take a moment to answer this question.

Have you ever sat aimlessly in your life with nothing to achieve, nowhere to go and nothing to do?

The answer is No. You and I have always been chasing goals and aims. We have one to go and another to follow. Until a year ago I had assigned a very big goal to myself. This goal made it impossible for me to sleep. My mind would be up trying to work ways and means to help me achieve it. I began working relentlessly towards achieving it. Everytime I faced failure, I felt the pain and despair. I was dejected 100 times and happy just once when I achieved this nonsensical goal. When I decided to assign myself another bigger benchmark I stumbled upon the concept of Apranahita (Aimlessness). And I said to myself,

'I'll give myself thirty days to be aimless and see what happens.' The result was happiness, bliss, a stress-free life. Mediocrity and modesty about doing nothing and not wanting to achieve anything and simply being in the moment. Do you get it, how important it is to Stop? How important it is to be aimless, to not do or run after something. If you haven't still understood this then give yourself fourteen days of aimlessness and see how it feels. I am certain you will write to me and share your blissful realizations.

There is immense power in being aimless. There is immense joy in doing nothing. I would like to share a short story I read in Thich Nhat Hanh's book. One day a farmer lost all his cows. They just fled on a stormy night. The farmer was perplexed and kept running from home to home, places to look for his cows. While looking he kept sharing the pain and loss he would suffer if he didn't get his cows back. While in search of his precious belonging he stumbled upon Buddha. Buddha was addressing his disciples and explaining the essence of aimlessness when he was interrupted by this worried and harried farmer. The farmer asked Buddha if he had seen his cows and Buddha replied with a No. To this the farmer ranted about his miserable life if he didn't find his prized possession. The Buddha felt very compassionate towards him but could not help him out of his misery. As the man left, Buddha turned to his disciples and said, 'Good we don't have the cows, as we don't need to be worried.'

This is what aimlessness does to you – you are never worried and you are never in a rush to go anywhere. You are just here and living the moment. I completely agree with the Buddhist approach to Apranahita. I know you will find it amusing to be aimless and goalless. Some of you may even laugh at me. But trust me, the best way to test this concept is to go aimless for a few days and see the results for yourself. Just keep all your goals aside and do what you do without any ambition, aspiration or goal. Just do something because you like it or feel passionately for not because it is going to take you some place or get you something. You need to stop like I did few years ago. I lead a very simple life – I love to spend time with my daughter, husband and dog. When a friend calls me I am always available. I always have the time to be with my parents and help them through old age and sickness. I always have the time to speak to my clients who are in distress and guide them through. I always have the time for a peaceful sleep and ten minutes of meditation. These are the rewards of going aimless and yet doing what you love to do. I love being a Tarot reader and a writer and nowhere have I compromised professionally or personally. I am just goalless, aimless and I am happy.

Hope you too choose happiness over misery. Realize the essence of impermanence (Anicca) and be aimless. Stop and look at the beauty of life and make time to bask in its glory. If you have any questions feel free to write to me at karmel@tarotreader. in and I'll do my best to clarify your doubts. For more interesting concepts and a better understanding of what I have written above I recommend you read a few or all of these titles listed below.

Books on Mindfulness Training

Mindfulness in Plain English by Bhante Henepola Gunaratana

You Are Here by Thich Naht Hanh

The Miracle of Mindfulness by Thich Naht Hanh

A Guide to Awareness by Somdet Phra Nyanasamvara

Being Peace by Thich Naht Hanh

Be Free Where You Are by Thich Naht Hanh

Intuitive Awareness by Ajahn Sumedho

Making Your Mind an Ocean by Venerable Lama Thubten Yeshe

Diamond Sutra by Osho Rajneesh

Talks on Vipassana Meditation by Ven. Sayadaw Kundala
Becoming your Own Therapist by Lama Thubten Yeshe
The Art of Living by Ven. Master Ching Kung
Practical Vipassana Meditation by Ven. Mahasi Sayadaw
Taming the Monkey Mind by Cheng Wei-an
Cutting Through Spiritual Materialism by Chogyam Trungpa
Lankavatara Sutra (Buddhanet.net)

With this I end my journey with you this year. I hope this book will give you all the clarity you need to overcome your apprehensions of the future, let go of the clutches of the past and harness your power by realizing the beauty of being, of living in the moment.

Acknowledgements

This book is a product of my hard work, knowledge of, and dedication to Tarot. I would like to thank the universe for giving me this opportunity for the third time to bring the magical power of Tarot to you in the form of this book. My mission is to make Tarot a household name and the universe has helped me in every aspect to achieve this.

I would like to thank my beloved husband Manoj Nair for his support and my daughter Miara for her patience and love. They are my pillars who have helped me become what I am today.

Finally, I would like to thank my publisher HarperCollins for giving me this brilliant opportunity to bring forth the magic of Tarot to you through this book.

Two other important people who have helped me with my books are Sucharita Dutta-Asane, the editor of my book who has worked with me on every project; my book is as much her success as mine. Bidisha Srivastava, for her relentless coordination that has taken my books across the seven seas. This book is a product of all our efforts. I hope you enjoy unravelling your future through it.

Acknowledgments

Other titles by Karmel Nair